Om morgonen billiga gå vi åter först-
gården till Giästgifvaren gärdom som nästig
trögt blev åtven, at fråga Giästgifvaren
efter hemlogi om Chan en hord, som skolat
gifst inladning; men Giästgifvaren var
borta, sedan vid krogen, drängen visade
Nordast åt er vägen och igenom vägen
och iust Kullen fördgy åtevarnat. Bengt
som allena efter oss vist de så niltn
mot uti en backe, jemte en Aplelid;
ehuru här var intet jorden, med-
någon Spada i längre tider jord, och
der var intet Barg. framtin åt ond da futtn på ett slut
Zi varom nögde sidan vi fik enters,
at den curieuse Faggot Inspectorn vid
Landrenteri Cantoratt finst unvit
vår Giästgifvaren, och legt befredt thm
ti den hen här inrättande Alun verne-
tet.
Talen liulvks här så orlen och Helm i
Kullent för nåferer, dock så, at Helmen si
intet Kuller den Kynd, och si avvie, som
et nåferas led, som vare Kelar för-
gnister, Kvid Kundsaten Kiivrnt Helmen
jemlvef, Et trvådn Kittst nnut, och si
inder litnt nåferer vid Ludergn
pet, ehr rögy livlas Helmen mnd nn
dubbl flodet Torf, da den indarstn
Torforen rvändr pi grvödmvie at
Helmen; men ehon åt Gintelen; Inttn
flar dock nj pi Cindinguit teltn.
Zi observerade pi hela Öland, at rvört
gröta Gud och bjre lvys Irngt nndnn för
landsbarnen rf vid Kabfentst nnde, Hr hn
. det eltps pi den mn sidnn Bulferen
och på len indnn rvngen och huf, teltfi/art

Endpapers: Two manuscript pages from Linnaeus's journals, from the collection of the Royal Linnean Society, London.

Opposite page: The first Swedish illustration of *Linnaea borealis*, from a woodcut by *Rudbeck the younger*.

Linnaeus

TRAVELS

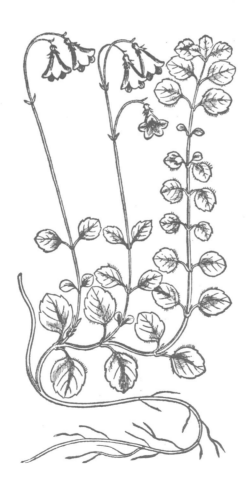

Linnaeus in his Lapland costume, a Mezzotint by *Dunkarton* after a painting
by *M. Hoffman*. (*Royal Linnean Society, London*).

Nature Classics

Carl Linnaeus
TRAVELS

Edited by David Black
Illustrated by Stephen Lee

CHARLES SCRIBNER'S SONS • NEW YORK

Copyright © 1979 The Felix Gluck Press Ltd., Twickenham, England
© 1973 Öland and Gotland Journey Translation by Marie Åsberg and William T. Stearn
Linnaean Classification © 1957 and 1971 W.T. Stearn

Library of Congress Cataloging in Publication Data
Linné, Carl von, 1701-1778.
Travels.

(Nature classics)
Includes index.
1. Linné, Carl von, 1707-1778. 2. Natural history—Sweden. 3. Natural history—Europe, Northern. 4. Sweden—Description and travel. 5. Europe, Northern—Description and travel. 6. Naturalists—Sweden—Biography. I. Black, David. II. Title. III. Series.
QH43.T7 1979   500.9485   79-13252

Printed in Germany (Federal Republic) by Konkordia GmbH 758 Bühl/Baden

Explanation of names used in the text

In this book the names used in the text are those used by Linnaeus in his original publications, although many of the long descriptive names have been shortened to the first phrase or word of the description. Where this has been done the name used is followed by 'etc.'

Vernacular names have been translated or transliterated, and where Linnaeus used a vernacular and a Latin name both have been included. Linnaeus's name for each organism is followed by its modern name within square brackets. For higher plants the common name only is used, with the exception of a few species which have none. For other organisms the modern scientific name is used together with a general common name (e.g., Lichen, moss).

At the time of his travels in Lapland, Öland and Gotland, Linnaeus had not yet developed the binomial system, and used Latin names which varied in length from one word for familiar species, e.g., *Caltha* (marsh marigold) and *Spergula* (corn spurrey), through two- and three-word phrases to long sentences used for new or unusual species; e.g. *Orchis bulbis indivisis, nectarii labio quinquefido punctis scabro, cornu obtuso, petalis distinctis* (military orchid). These descriptive names are cumbersome and Linnaeus did not use them consistently. Thus, fly orchid first appears (Öland, 2 June) as *Cypripedium bulbis subrotundis, foliis oblongis caulinis* but on 13 June the same species is called *Orchis muscam referens*.

Linnaeus first used binomial nomenclature in the index of *Öländska och Gothländska Resa* from which extracts have been taken for this book. This takes the form of a binomial together with a number which is a reference to the plant's full description in *Flora Suecica*; e.g., *Euphorbia 438 Oelandica* (marsh spurge).

The editor and publishers would like to thank Professor W.T. Stearn and the Linnaean Society for their help and advice and for permission to use the text published in the Society's *Biological Journal* vol. 19 as a basis for the Öland and Gotland sections.

They are also grateful to Professor Stearn for allowing them to use part of his publications on Linnaean classification, originally published in his *Introduction to the Species Plantarum* and in W. Blunt's *The Compleat Naturalist*.

1 3 5 7 9 11 13 15 17 19 I/C 20 18 16 14 12 10 8 6 4 2

Contents

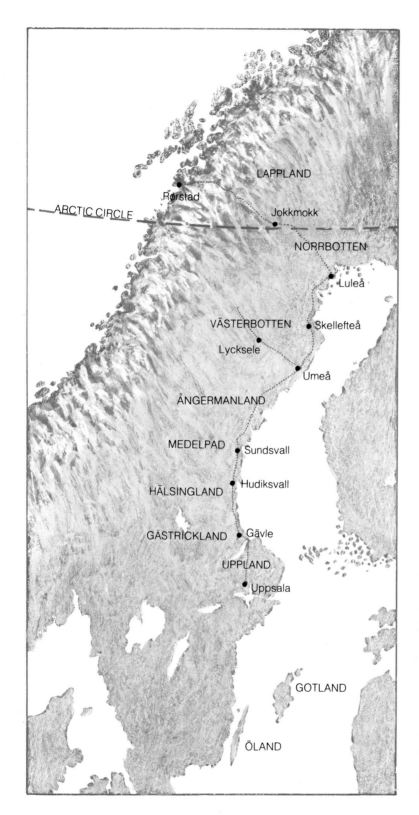

LAPPLAND

ARCTIC CIRCLE

Rørstad

Jokkmokk

NÖRRBOTTEN

Luleå

VÄSTERBOTTEN

Skellefteå

Lycksele

Umeå

ÅNGERMANLAND

MEDELPAD

Sundsvall

HÄLSINGLAND

Hudiksvall

GÄSTRICKLAND

Gävle

UPPLAND

Uppsala

GOTLAND

ÖLAND

Map of Sweden
The old place-names from the time of Linnaeus are in brackets next to the new names on this list. In the text we have followed English usage for the spelling of 'Lapland'.

Uppsala (Upsala)
Gävle (Gefle)
Jockmokk (Jockmock)

Lappland (Lapland)
Västerbotten (Westbothnia)
Hälsingland (Helsingland)
Gästrikland (Gestrickland)
Uppland (Upland)
Gotland (Gothland)

Introduction

At the time of Linnaeus's birth, Sweden was a powerful nation. Its territory included not only Sweden itself but also Finland and part of north-western Russia (the Leningrad region, then called Ingria), Estonia and Latvia (then called Livland), and the Stettin and Bremen regions of northern Germany. Its young king, Carl XII, from 1699 until his death in 1718 fought brilliantly and ceaselessly against his neighbours the Danes, Russians, Saxons and Poles to keep his Baltic empire. Quite naturally, Linnaeus's parents named their first-born son Carl after their victorious monarch. But the wars exhausted Sweden, and Linnaeus grew up in a nation impoverished but intent on recovery.

Linnaeus (or von Linné) was born in 1707 in Småland, a south-eastern province of Sweden. The people of the province have long had a reputation for resourcefulness, tenacity and thrift. His father, Nils Ingemarsson, a clergyman, had coined the surname Linnaeus for himself in commemoration of a huge linden tree (Tilia cordata), known in the Småland dialect as a 'linn'.

Nils Linnaeus was a keen gardener, and Carl soon acquired from him a love of flowers and gardening. The rectory garden must have been one of the best in Sweden and Nils followed the fashion of the time by making the centrepiece of his garden a raised circular flower-bed, an imitation dining-room table planted with shrubs, herbs and flowering plants which represented the dishes on the table as well as the various guests. As a toddler Linnaeus would amuse himself in the garden playing with flowers rather than proper toys.

Twinflower *Linnaea borealis*

When he was just four years old he was taken along on a picnic to the nearby lake Möckeln. Here his father expounded to his guests the names of the many wild flowers found along the shores; the child was so fascinated with the names that from that moment he pestered his father to repeat them. His father, seemingly a patient man, told the young boy that he would not fill his head with new names until he had learned the old ones. And so was kindled the interest in the naming of plants and animals which dominated Linnaeus's life and gives us cause to remember him today.

His schooldays were not the happiest, for school discipline was harsh, the lessons were long (beginning at 6 a.m. and ending at 5 p.m.) and the subjects taught were little to his taste. Three-quarters of the time was devoted to Latin, Greek and theology;

pupils had to use Latin not only in conversation with their teachers but between themselves. He began his schooling at Växjö, the cathedral town about 30 miles (50 km) from his home at Stenbrohult, in 1714, at the age of seven, and finished in 1727. Luckily he found an ally in the headmaster, Daniel Lannerus. Linnaeus's father and maternal grandfather had both been clergymen, and naturally his mother hoped he would become one too. She was grievously disappointed when he showed no vocation for it and wished to become a physician instead. Thanks to the support and encouragement of Johan Rothman, a state doctor, his parents allowed him to study medicine and in August he enrolled at the university of Lund, the capital of the province. Though he stayed there for less than a year, he had the good fortune to be befriended by a kindly and generous professor, Kilian Stobaeus, who let him live in his house, lent him books and instructed him in natural history. But he became ill and had to return home. On Rothman's advice he decided to renew his studies at Uppsala, four hundred miles to the north.

Conditions it seemed were uncongenial for study, but Linnaeus was so determined that it seemed inevitable he would make an early breakthrough as one of the leading students in the natural sciences. He achieved this through a rather clever dissertation on the sexuality of plants, 'Praeludia Sponsalarium Plantarum', in which he described the functions of the stamens and pistils in pollination. He equated pollen with sperm and seeds with the ova or egg. This provocative subject, with its implications of incest and polygamy, was to earn Linnaeus a doubtful reputation among the more conservative members of society. But his teachers appreciated the clear, eloquent style and originality of content. He worked hard in these early years, passionately devoted to his subject. It was during this time that he embarked on his important works, including the Bibliotheca Botanica and Genera Plantarum.

At Uppsala Linnaeus met a student from the north, Petrus Artedi, who shared his interest in natural history. Artedi was slightly older and much more learned and thorough, and he had a knowledge of languages which Linnaeus never acquired. Together they made an agreement to record the whole realm of nature in an orderly methodical manner; if one of them died, the duty of completing this enormous task would fall upon the other. In 1735 Artedi was drowned tragically in a canal in Amsterdam, and Linnaeus was left with the task of publishing his work on fishes and pursuing their ambitious plan alone.

In 1731 Linnaeus went home to Småland. He had been away for three years and things at the university were not going too well. A rival had returned from abroad and Linnaeus decided to take a welcome break. He discussed with his family his progress and his plans, amongst them a proposed visit to Lapland. His mother was, it seems, worried about him going; but his father gave him encouragement. 'If you are confident that this journey will advance your career, then ask God for guidance and help. He is everywhere, even among the wildest fells. Trust in Him. My prayers will go with you.'

Before leaving Uppsala, Linnaeus had approached the Royal Society of Sciences of Uppsala for financial assistance for the trip. On his return to university his eagerness and persistence were rewarded, and the Society granted him a sum of 450 copper dalers, two-thirds of what he had originally asked for. He set out alone on horseback on 12 May 1732 full of hope. His brief was to record as much as possible of the natural history, agriculture and customs of Lapland and its people. His route ran northwards along a well-ridden track to the town of Umeå; from there it took him inland and westwards into Lycksele Lapland, back north to the coast, then inland once again into Luleå Lapland and over the mountains into Norway; finally south and east along the Gulf of Bothnia, which was then Swedish territory. (He seems to have met some Finns on the way, but his account of them is not too flattering.) The journey took four months in all. He returned almost worn out but enriched by his

experience, loaded with numerous observations and species. The botanical results were published as the Flora Lapponica *in Amsterdam in 1737. It is unfortunate for his contemporaries that his original journal,* Iter Lapponica, *was not published until 1888 although a translation into English had been made from his unpublished manuscript and appeared in 1811 under the title* Lachesis Lapponica *or* A Tour in Lapland, *because it is truly fascinating in its description of miscellaneous findings.*

Linnaeus may have exaggerated the difficulties of his journey but in turn he gives us great insight into the strange customs of the Lapps: uses of reindeer milk, cures for chilblains, and how to play 'tablut' – a cross between chess and draughts with Swedes and Russians as the pieces. He also illustrated his journal with drawings of plants, insects, the Lapps, and expressionistic sketches of himself among the northern wilderness.

Linnaeus made altogether four major expeditions within Sweden. The first, the Lapland journey, at the age of twenty-five, the second to the Baltic islands of Öland and Gotland when he was thirty-four and the final provincial tours to Västergotland and Skåne when he was in his late forties. He also travelled to Holland, England and France. He died, full of honours, in 1778. His library and herbarium were shortly afterwards bought and transferred to England, where they are housed in the rooms of the Linnaean Society in London.

Journey to Lapland

I set out alone from the city of Uppsala on Friday, 12 May 1732, at 11 o'clock, being at that time within half a day of twenty-five years of age.

At this season nature wore her most cheerful and delightful aspect.

> Spring clothes the fields and decks the flowery grove,
> And all creation glows with life and love.

Now the winter corn was a quarter ell high and the barley had just shot out its blade. The birch, the elm and the aspen tree began to put forth their leaves.

I had no sooner passed the northern gate of the city than I perceived signs of clay soil, except in the hills, which consist of sand and stones. The road here is level, and for a quarter of a mile destitute of trees. In ditches by the wayside the water byssus (an algae) was observed, particularly in places sheltered from the wind. It greatly resembles the cream of milk, and is called by the peasants 'water flower'.

Among the few wayside plants now in flower were *Taraxacum* [dandelion], *Draba caule nudo longitudine palm* [common whitlow-grass] which in Småland is called 'Rågblomma' [rye flower] because as soon as the husbandman sees it in bloom he is accustomed to sow his Lent corn; *Thlaspi* [field pennycress], *Myosotidem* [water forget-menot], *Viola arv* [field pansy] and *Primula* [cowslip]. Also *Caltha* [marsh marigold], sometimes known here as 'Svensk capris' [Swedish caper] as many people are said to eat it instead of the true caper; the report of its giving colour to butter is certainly false.

The lark was my companion all the way, flying before me, quivering in the air.

16

1 Marsh Marigold *Caltha palustris*
2 Wild pansy *Viola tricolor*
3 Sweet Violet *Viola odorata*
4 Cowslip *Primula veris*
5 Water Forgetmenot *Myosotis scorpioides*
6 Field Pennycress *Thlaspi arvense*

Gästrikland to Medelpad

At Högsta, a mile and a quarter from Uppsala, the forests began to thicken. The charming lark here left me; but another bird welcomed my approach to the forest, namely *Turdus minor* [redwing] whose amorous warblings from the tops of the spruce trees were no less delightful.

13 May

The forest abounded with *Anemonoides* [wood anemone], the *Hepatica* [hepatica] and *Oxys* [wood sorrel]. Their blossoms were all closed. Who has endowed plants with intelligence, to shut themselves up at the approach of rain? Even when the weather changes in a moment from sunshine to rain, though before expanded, they immediately close. Here for the first time this season I heard the cuckoo, a welcome harbinger of summer.

Here also I beheld a plant I had never before met with in our northern regions, namely *Pulsatilla apii folio* [pale pasque flower], the leaves of which, furnished with long footstalks, had two pairs of leaflets besides the terminal one, every one of them cut halfway into four, six or eight segments. The calyx, if I may be allowed so to call it, was placed about the middle of the stalk, and was cut into numerous very narrow divisions, smooth within, very hairy without. Petals six, oblong; the outermost excessively hairy and purplish, all of them white on the inside with purple veins. Stamens numerous and very short.

We had variable weather, with alternate rain and sunshine.

A mile from Älvkarleby are iron works called Harnäs. These were burnt down by the Russians, but have since been repaired.

Here runs the river which divides the provinces of Uppland and Gästrikland. The post houses and inns are dreadfully bad.

The forests became more and more hilly and stony, and abounded with different species of *Pyrolae* [wintergreen].

Round-leaved Wintergreen *Pyrola rotundifolia*

18

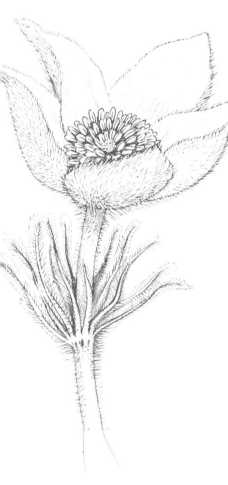

Pale Pasque Flower *Pulsatilla*

I had scarcely passed the limits of Hälsingland when I perceived two *Lagopodes* [willow grouse] in the road, but could not get near enough to fire at them. Viewed through my spying glass, they appeared for the most part of a reddish cast, but the wing feathers were a snowy white.

The highest mountain in Medelpad according to the locals is called Norbykullen. It is indeed of a very considerable height; and being desirous of examining it more minutely, I travelled to Norrbyn, tied my horse up and, accompanied by a guide, climbed the mountain on its left side. Here were many uncommon plants, including *Moschatel* [moschatel].

After much difficulty and fatigue we reached the summit of the mountain and looked down on a wide vista of plains and cultivated fields, villages, lakes and rivers.

The dung of the hare was seen all over the highest part of the hill, proof that this animal frequents even these lofty regions.

We endeavoured to descend on the south side, which was the steepest. We were often obliged to sit down, and in that position to slide for a considerable way. About the middle of the way down, a *Bubo* [eagle owl] started up suddenly before us. It was as large as a hen and the colour of a woodcock, with black feathery ears or horns. Later we found both eggs and young of this great bird.

Here and there among the rocks sprouted small patches of plants, including *Violas tricoloras* [wild pansy], of which some of the flowers were white, others blue and white, others blue and yellow or a mixture of all. All these were found within half an ell of each other, sometimes on the same stalk; a plain proof that such diversities do not constitute a specific distinction.

Ångermanland

19 May

In the heart of the Ångermannian forests, trees with deciduous leaves, *Betula* [silver birch] and the *Alnus alba* [alder], abound equally with *Pinus* [scots pine] and *Abietes* [Norway spruce] while among the humble shrubs the *Erica* [heather] and *Vaccinia* [bilberry] alternately predominate; the former chiefly on the hills, the latter in the closer parts of the forest.

Not far from Äskja the little *Rubus fragariae folio* [arctic bramble] was in full bloom. The cold weather, however, had rendered the purple of its blossoms paler than usual.

Having taken leave of the mountain Skuleberget, I had scarcely continued my journey a quarter of a mile before I found a great part of the country covered with snow. The pretty spring flowers had gradually disappeared. The buds of the birch, which so greatly contribute to the beauty of the forests, were not yet put forth. I saw nothing but wintry plants, the *Erica* [heather] and the *Vaccinia* [bilberry] peeping through the snow.

24 May

The ground here is tolerably level; the soil sand, sometimes clay. In some places are large tracts of moss. The whole country, owing to the sand and the moss, is by no means fertile, though it affords a good deal of milk.

I waited on Baron Grundell, governor of Umeå province, who received me in the kindest manner. He had in a cage two *Loxias* [crossbills] which fed with great dexterity on the cones of spruce. They took up a cone with their beak and, holding it fast with one foot, picked out the seeds by means of their forked mandibles, of which the upper is very thick, ending in an oblong, curved, very sharp point. From his window I perceived in an adjoining fen the *Motacilla flava* [yellow wagtail] and *Hirunduines* [swallows].

Birch *Betula alba*

left Scots Pine *Pinus sylvestris*
right Norway Spruce *Picea abies*

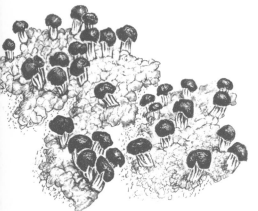

Lichen uncialis L. = Cladonia uncialis

Lichen lyssoides L. = Baeomyces rufus

Lichen cocciferus L. = Cladonia coccifera

The route to Lycksele

I took leave of Umeå. The weather was rainy and continued so the whole day. I turned out of the main road to the left, my design being to visit Lycksele Lappmarken. The road grew more and more narrow and bad so that my horses went stumbling along at almost every step. In this dreary wilderness I began to feel very solitary, and to long earnestly for a companion.

In the evening I arrived at Jämtböl. On my enquiring what I could have for supper, they set before me the breast of a male capercaillie that had been shot and dressed some time the preceding year. Its aspect was not inviting, and I imagined the flavour would not be much better, but in this respect I was mistaken. The taste proved delicious, and I wondered at the ignorance of those who, having more fowls than they know how to dispose of, suffer many of them to be spoiled, as often happens in Stockholm.

27 May

Rain prevented me from pursuing my journey till noon. Even then all the elements were against me. In every direction the branches of the trees hung down before my eyes, loaded with raindrops.

Here and there, in the heart of the forests, were level, healthy spots where I found the perforated *Muscus coralloides* [lichen; *Cladonia rangiferina*] and another kind very similar but as thick as one's finger, snow-white and with more copious, and dense entangled branches [*Cladonia rangiferina var alpestris*]. There was also an elegant cup moss [lichen; *Cladonia coccifera*] and everywhere on the road grew the *Muscus lichenoides foliosum caninum sulphureum* [lichen; *Nephroma arcticum*].

Wherever I came I could get nothing to drink but water. Against the walls of the houses the *Agaricus pedis equini facie* [Fungus; *Phellinus ignarius*] was hung up to serve as a pin cushion.

22

Very early in the morning I quitted Granön in a 'hååp', a small boat. We proceeded to Lycksele. When the sun rose, nothing could be more pleasant than the view of this clear unruffled stream. As we made our way we passed several small islets where we saw many ringed plovers and sandpipers. Cranes are also found here. The rower said he had shot one and nailed it up against the wall with all its feathers on. What an absurdity!

Lichen nivalis L. = *Cetraria nivalis*

30 May

The pasture ground near the parsonage of Lycksele was very poor but quite the reverse a quarter of a mile distant. Here the butter was extremely remarkable for its fine yellow colour, approaching almost to a reddish or saffron hue. On my enquiring what kinds of herbs most abounded in these pastures, the people gave me a description of one which I judged to be *Melampyrum* [cow-wheat].

31 May

At Whitsuntide this year no Laplander was at church, the pikes happening to spawn just at that time. This fishery constitutes the chief trade of these people, and they were therefore now for the most part dispersed among the alps, each in his own tract.

The eatable moss of Norway *Lichen islandicus* [lichen; *Cetraria islandica*] was here of two kinds or varieties, one broad and scattered, the other in thick tufts about 3 inches high.

In the neighbouring forest grew a rare little leafy lichen *Lichen croceus* [*Solorina crocea*] of a fine saffron colour beneath, and bearing on the upper side flat oblong shields; also the fungus *Boletus perennis* [*coltricha perennis*].

This part of the country is beautifully diversified with hills and valleys, clothed with forests of birch intermixed with fir, which were now reflected by the calm surface of the water. By the shore grew *Equisetum nudum seu aphyllum* [Dutch rush] and behind large stands of *Juncello aquatico* [deer-grass].

Like all people addicted to fishing, the Laplanders are very fond of brandy.

Lichen islandicus L. = *Cetraria islandica*

Lichen croceus L. = *Solorina crocea*

Along the river

We pursued our journey by water with considerable labour and difficulty all night long, if it might be called night which was as light as the day, the sun disappearing for about half an hour only.

In the evening we came to an island occupied by fishermen. The fish they collected was chiefly pike, with some char (*Salmo alpinus*). The fat parts, with the intestines, after having been cleaned, are put together until they become sour, then an oil is obtained for the purpose of greasing shoes. The spawn is dried and afterwards used in bread, dumplings, and in a sort of gruel made by boiling flour or oatmeal in milk or water.

2 June

We continued our course up the river of Umeå. At length, quitting the main stream, we proceeded along a branch to the right, which bears the name of Juktån.

I observed *Erica* [heather], large cowberries, *Empetri baccae* [crowberries] and *Myrtillus baccis nigris* [bilberry],

24

1 Bilberry *Vaccinium myrtillus*
2 Crowberry *Empetrum nigrum*
3 Heather *Calluna vulgaris*
4 Cowberry *Vaccinium vitis-idaea*
5 Crane *Grus grus*

but what pleased and surprised me most was a little *Viola tricolor lutea* etc. [yellow wood-violet] which has not been observed before in Sweden.

We waited till about 2 o'clock in the afternoon for the return of the Laplander whom I had sent on an expedition. He was accompanied by a person whose appearance was such that I did not know whether I beheld a man or a woman. A woman it was, whose face was the darkest brown from the effect of smoke. Her pitchy-coloured hair hung loose about her head and on it she wore a flat red cap. She had a grey petticoat; and from her neck, which resembled the skin of a frog, were suspended a pair of large loose breasts of the same brown complexion but encompassed by way of ornament with brass rings. Her first aspect really struck me with dread; but though a fury in appearance, she addressed me with mingled pity and reserve.

My health and strength being by this time naturally impaired, I enquired of this woman whether she could give me any food. She replied 'nothing but fish'. I looked at the fresh fish as it was called, but perceiving its mouth to be full of maggots, I had no appetite to touch it. I asked if I could have any reindeer tongues, but was answered in the negative. 'Have you any cheese made of reindeer's milk?' said I. 'Yes,' she replied, 'but it is a mile off.' 'Would you allow me to buy some?' 'I have no desire', answered the good woman, 'that thou shouldst die in my country for want of food.'

Angelica *Angelica sylvestris*

Retreat to Umeå

The reindeer suffers great hardship in autumn, when the snow being all melted away during summer, a sudden frost freezes the *Muscus coralloides perforatum* [lichen; *Cladonia rangiferina*] that is his only winter food. When this fails, the animal has no other resources, for he never touches hay. His keepers fell the trees in order to supply him with the filamentous lichens that clothe their branches. But this kind of food does not supply the place of what is natural to him.

The reindeer feeds also on frogs, snakes, and even on the Norwegian lemming, often pursuing the latter to so great a distance as not to find his way back again.

I here satisfied myself about the native species of *Angelica*, which are two only, not three – angelica and garden angelica.

The bountiful provision of nature is evinced in providing mankind with bed and bedding even in this savage wilderness. The *Polytrichum prolif. maximum* [great hair moss; *Polytrichum commune*] grows copiously in the damp forests and is used for this purpose. They choose the starry-headed plants, out of the tufts of which they cut a surface as large as they please for bed or bolster, separating it from the earth beneath. This mossy cushion is very soft and elastic; and if a similar portion of it be made into a coverlet, nothing can be more warm and comfortable.

7 June

Early in the morning I left Granön and in passing through the forest I picked up a curious insect, *Cantharis niger maculatus et undulatus* [wood tiger beetle; *Cicindela sylavatica*], which I met with in great abundance in this province.

26

above Reindeer Moss *Cladonia rangiferina*
below Great Hair Moss *Polytrichum commune*

Near the town of Umeå, in a springy spot on the side of a hill, I met with three or four curious mosses.

1. A kind of moss (*Hypnum* or *Polytrichum*) with branched stem bearing flowers in the form of shields. (The male plant of *Phillinotis fontana*.)

From the root arises an oblique stem about ½ inch in length, entirely clothed with very sharp-pointed leaves. From thence the main stem grows perpendicularly to the height of one inch, of a purple colour, clothed with ovate, acute, whitish scales, each half embracing the stem. At the summit of the main stem stands a sort of blossom composed of six scales. It is curious that all the flowers, in each tuft composed perhaps of a hundred plants, rise exactly to the same level.

2. This moss (the female plant of *Bartramia fontana*) differs from the first in the following particulars. The roots or shoots of the preceding year are quite black, while those of the present season are of a paler or whitish green. The plants are also more branched and less curved. In the last place this is a fruit-bearing kind, having purple stalks 2 inches long, each with a globular head, larger than usual in mosses and of a green colour.

3. This is a moss [*Bryum binum*] whose stems and leaves are of a blood-red hue and are regularly and alternately imbricated, oblong, pointed; the upper ones forming a head at the summits of the branches as in No. 1, but the disk not exposed. This therefore is the male and No. 4 the female found on the same plant. The latter bears on a long stalk, greenish at the upper part, an oblong pear-shaped capsule. The veil is very small.

At the same place as these mosses I caught a large kind of gnat, *Culex ibidem maximus* [*Tipula rivosa*].

11 June

Being Sunday and a day of continued rain, I remained at Umeå.

left drawing of *Andromeda polifolia* by Linnaeus

Andromeda polifolia

12 June

Erica palustris pendula etc. [bog rosemary] was in its highest beauty, decorating the marshy grounds in a most agreeable manner. The flowers are quite blood-red before they expand, but when full-grown the corolla is of a flesh colour. Scarcely any painter's art can so happily imitate the beauty of a fine female complexion; still less could any artificial colour upon the face itself bear a comparison with this lovely blossom.

As I contemplated it, I could not help thinking of Andromeda as described by the poets; if these poets had had the little plant in view they could scarcely have contrived a more apposite fable. Andromeda is represented by them as a virgin of most exquisite and unrivalled charms; but these charms remain in perfection only so long as she retains her virgin purity, which is so applicable to the plant, now preparing to celebrate its nuptuals. This plant is always fixed on some little turfy hillock in the midst of the swamps, as Andromeda herself was chained to a rock in the sea, which bathed her feet as the fresh water does the roots of the plant. Dragons and venomous serpents surrounded her, as toads and other reptiles frequent the abode of her vegetable prototype, and, when they pair in the spring, throw mud and water over its leaves and branches. As the distressed virgin cast down her blushing face through excessive affliction, so does the rosy-coloured flower hang its head, growing paler and paler till it withers away.

Hence, as this plant forms a new genus, I have chosen for it the name *Andromeda*.

Flora found growing in a Sphagnum Moss bog
1 Bog Rosemary *Andromeda polifolia*
2 Cranberry *Vaccinium oxycoccus*
3 Dwarf Birch *Betula nana*
4 Hare's Tail *Eriophorum vaginatum*
5 Crowberry *Empetrum nigrum*
6 Cloudberry *Rubus chamaemorus*
7 Northern Bilberry *Vaccinium uliginosum*
8 Mushroom *Lyophyllum palustre*
9 Sphagnum Moss
10 Mosquito
11 Female Wolf Spider with egg sac

Old Piteå

left Common Butterwort
Pinguicula vulgaris
below Bogbean *Menyanthes trifoliata*

13 June

In the neighbourhood grows *Pinguicula* [common butter-wort]. When the inhabitants of these parts once procure this plant, they avail themselves of it throughout the whole year; for they preserve it dried during the winter; and use it as a kind of rennet till the return of spring.

The fields in this part of the countryside are excellent. The crops are usually abundant, provided the corn be not injured by frost, as it had been the preceding year. Owing to this misfortune, I found bread made of spruce fir bark in general use. The *Menyanthes* [bogbean] is very seldom used on account of its bitterness.

14 June

An owl appeared, flitting every now and then at short distances before me. Laying hold of my gun, I ventured to take aim, though my horse kept going on at a good rate. It was a quarter past twelve at night, though not at all dark. I was lucky enough to hit the bird, but in such a manner that one side of it was too damaged to allow of stuffing it. This was *Noctua dorso fusco* etc. [hawk owl]. Just as I was

30

about to draw up a description of this owl, a little beetle crept out of its plumage. By its antennae it was evidently a scarab. The whole body was oblong, shaded with blue or black; the belly white.

15 June

The next evening, a little before the sun went down, I was assailed by such multitudes of gnats as surpass all imagination. They seemed to occupy the whole atmosphere, especially when I travelled through low or damp meadows. They filled my mouth, nose and eyes. Luckily they did not bite or sting, though they almost choked me.

Just at sunset I reached the town of Old Piteå. Near the landing spot stood a gibbet with a couple of wheels on which lay the bodies of two Finlanders without heads. These men had been executed for highway robbery and murder. They were accompanied by the quartered body of a Laplander who had murdered one of his relations.

Immediately on entering the town I procured a lodging, but had not been long in bed before I perceived a glare of light on the wall of my chamber. I was alarmed by the idea of fire, but on looking out of the window saw the sun rising, perfectly red, which I did not expect to take place so soon. The cock crowed, the birds began to sing, and sleep was banished from my eyelids.

19 June

The people hereabouts talked much of mountains haunted by hobgoblins; also of seas and fishing places where nothing is to be caught unless by those who come unexpectedly.

On the island of Långön, three miles from Old Piteå, I was lucky enough to find growing under a spruce tree the *Corallorhiza* [coralroot] in full bloom. It is a very rare plant. The root is throughout of the thickness of a very small quill, white, smooth, fleshy, almost horizontal, branched and subdivided like a coral.

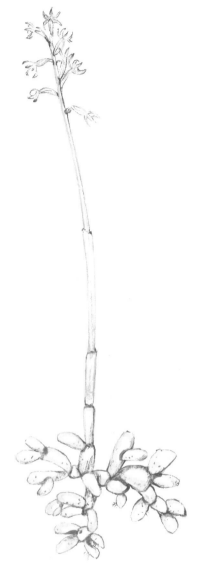

above Coral Root *Corallorhiza trifida*
below Linnaean drawing of Hawk
Owl *Surnia ulula*

District of Luleå

21 June

I took my leave of the old town of Piteå and arrived at the more modern one of Luleå.

The bogs were now white with the tufts of both kinds of *Moarna* the 'upright' harestail and 'pendulous' common cotton-grass. The marshes were clothed with the white blossoms of *Ledum* [Labrador tea].

The forests were also white with *Trientalis* [chickweed wintergreen] scattered with the small yellow flowers of *Melampyrum* [small cow-wheat] and mauve *Geranium* [wood cranesbill]. The meadows were perfectly yellow with *Ranunculus erectus* [meadow buttercup] and some of the cornfields were no less so with *Brassica campestris* [turnip].

I noted the arborescent willow *Salix arb foliis laro cerasi* [tea-leaved willow], whose leaves are like laurel. It is remarkable for the undulations or flexures between the serratures of the leaf. Other species of this tree, which grew in many forms, were *Salix arb foliis ulmi* [goat willow], *Salix arb foliis lauri latifolii* [bay willow] and *Salix pumila* etc. [*Salix myrtilloides*].

Another type, a shrubby willow with lanceolate downy leaves *Salix frutescens foliis, aeleagni lanceolatis, villosus* [downy willow], is rather a large shrub, but rarely rises to the size of a tree.

23 June

This day and the two preceding, indeed every day since the 18th, had been bright, warm and for the most part calm. The meadows were still fine and beautiful in their aspect, and everything conspired to favour the health and pleasure of the beholder. If the summer be indeed shorter here than in any other part of the world, it must be allowed, at the same time, to be nowhere more delightful. I was never in my life in better health than at present.

Ground flora of a damp Birch woodland
1 Wood Cranesbill *Geranium sylvaticum*
2 Fungus *Boletus* species
3 Grass of Parnassus *Parnassia palustris*
4 Arctic Bramble *Rubus arcticus*
5 Dwarf Cornel *Cornus suecica*
6 Labrador Tea *Ledum palustre*

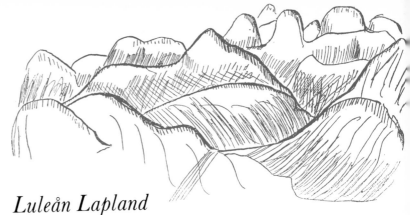

Three new plants Linnaeus encountered in Lapland
above Sibbaldia *Sibbaldia procumbens*
below Alpine Fleabane *Erigeron alpinus*
opposite Mountain Avens *Dryas octopetala* (in final fruiting phase)

Luleån Lapland

28 June

Near Storbacken, at the confluence of the great and small rivers of Luleå, is the boundary between Lappmarken and Västerbotten. After much trouble and fatigue I at length reached Jokkmokk, where stands the principal church of this northern district.

30 June

The clergyman Mr Malming, who is also the schoolmaster, and Mr Högling the curate tormented me with their consummate and most pertinacious ignorance. I could not but wonder how so much pride and ambition, such scandalous want of information, with such incorrigible stupidity, could exist in persons of their profession.

The 'learned' curate began his conversation with remarks on the clouds in this country, setting forth how they strike the mountains as they pass, carrying away stones, trees and cattle. I ventured to suggest that such accidents were rather to be attributed to the force of the wind, for that the clouds could not lift, or carry away, anything. He laughed at me, saying surely I had never seen any clouds. For my part, it seemed to me that he could have never been anywhere but in the clouds. Our conversation continued on other natural phenomena and at length he graciously advised me to pay some regard to the opinions of people skilled in these abstruse matters, and not, at my return home, to expose myself by publishing such absurd and preposterous opinions as I had now advanced.

The other, the pedagogue, lamented that people (like myself) should bestow so much attention upon temporal vanities, and consequently, alas, neglect their spiritual good. The number of pupils under the care of these gentlemen fortunately amounted to four only.

34

left Linnaean drawing of the Lulean Lapland Alps

The use of milk among the inhabitants of Västerbotten is very great; and the following are the various forms in which it serves them for food.

1. Fresh, of which a great deal is taken in the course of the day.

2. Fresh boiled.

3. Fresh boiled and coagulated with beer.

4. Sour milk deprived of its cream and capable of being cut.

5. Sourmilk eaten with its cream.

6. Butter made, as usual, of cream shaken till its oily part separates and floats.

7. Buttermilk – what remains after the butter is made.

8. Cheese made of fresh milk heated, coagulated with calves' rennet, then deprived of its whey and dried.

9. This whey having been boiled, the scum which rises is repeatedly collected.

10. The remaining whey is used instead of milk or water in making bread.

11. The same fluid, kept for a long time till it becomes viscid, is preserved through the winter.

12. The whey of cheese, boiled to a thick consistency, is then dried and stored in casks for use as an ingredient in the making of bread.

13. 'Sweet cheese' – made of fresh milk boiled till it is partly wasted and is the thickness of gruel; it is eaten fresh.

14. 'Meal cheese' – milk coagulated with rennet, mixed with meal and boiled.

15. Fresh milk poured on leaves of butterwort.

16. 'Napkin milk' – made by taking the thick substance of sour milk and hanging it up in a napkin to allow the liquid part to drain away.

17. Gäs-mjölk' – made by setting buttermilk in a tub till it begins to ferment, when fresh milk is added. The whey that forms at the bottom is drawn off and fresh milk again added, this procedure being repeated from time to time for about two weeks, till the milk becomes thick and excellent to eat.

18. Milk mixed with sorrel leaves and preserved till winter in the stomach of a reindeer, or some other animal.

1 Yellow Wood Violet *Viola biflora*
2 Moss Campion *Silene acaulis*
3 Alpine Mouse-ear *Cerastium alpinum*
4 Alpine Catchfly *Lychnis alpina*
5 Cassiope *Cassiope hypnoides*
6 Mat Grass *Nardus stricta*
7 Diapensia *Diapensia lapponica*
8 Mountain Avens *Dryas octopetala*
9 Purple Saxifrage *Saxifraga oppositifolia*
10 Roseroot *Rhodiola rosea*
11 Glacier Buttercup *Ranunculus glacialis*
12 Rough-legged Buzzard *Buteo lagopus*
13 Dotterel *Eudromias morinellus*

The Lapland alps

Other Lapland plants

above Drooping Saxifrage *Saxifraga cernua*
below Yellow Saxifrage *Saxifraga aizoides*

1 July

When I came to lake Skalka on the way towards Tjåmotis, I was struck with an opening between the hills through which appeared a range of mountains. Their summits reached the clouds, and indeed they resembled a range of white clouds rising from the horizon. In a word, I now beheld the Lapland alps.

Arriving in the evening at Tjåmotis, I saw the sun set apparently on the summit of a high mountain called Harrevarto. This spectacle I considered as not one of the least of nature's miracles. O Lord, how wonderful are thy works!

7 July

After having walked four or five miles in the course of the night, I went to sleep in the morning in one of the cottages of the country.

The inhabitants, sixteen in number, lay there all naked. They washed themselves by rubbing the body downwards, not upwards. They washed their dishes with their fingers, squirting water out of their mouths upon the spoon, then pouring into them boiled reindeer's milk, which was as thick as common milk mixed with eggs and had a strong flavour. Some thousands of reindeer came home in the morning; these were milked by men as well as women, who kneeled down on one knee.

My hosts gave me 'missen' to eat; that is whey after the curd is separated from it, coagulated by boiling, which renders it very firm. Its flavour was good, but the washing of the spoon took away my appetite, as the master of the house wiped it dry with his fingers, whilst his wife cleaned the bowl, in which milk had been in a similar manner, licking her fingers after every stroke.

I gathered this day some of the following plants.

Drooping saxifrage (*Saxifraga cernua*), which has one white flower at the top of the stem.

A very small *Pedicularis*, *Pedicularis flammea*. The leaves are brownish, pinnate; their segments imbricated. Flowers four, five, or more, at the top of the stem. Petal with an erect upper lip, which is narrow, compressed and brownish; the lower lip is horizontal, three-cleft, saffron-coloured like all the rest of the flower.

Yellow mountain saxifrage (*Saxifraga aizoides*). Flower yellow with large, flat calyx in five ovate segments.

'Michelia' (*Azalea lapponica*), which has an inconspicuous, green calyx in five obtuse segments. Petal one, erect, gradually dilated upwards, divided almost down to the base into five ovate segments, purple, deciduous.

Campanula uniflora, which differs from the harebell (*C. rotundifolia*) in having the leaves as well as the flower much contracted at the base, so that the latter is funnel-shaped.

A *Lychnis* with a concealed flower, *Lychnis apetala*. Flower solitary at the top of the stalk. Petals five, oblong, brownish, shaped exactly like the usual claws of a *Lychnis*, but without any border. The petals, stamens and pistils are all concealed within the calyx.

above Moor-king *Pedicularis flammea*
below Norwegian Lemming
Lemmus lemmus

The Öland and Gotland journeys

Linnaeus's Öland and Gotland journeys are little known outside his native Sweden. They are interesting not only because they cover the natural history, agriculture and archaeology of two Baltic islands then little known, but also because in the index to the published account of these journeys called Öländska och Gothländska Resa *he first used two-word names for species as alternatives to long descriptive names less easy to remember. The binomial system of nomenclature which he later used consistently for all the known plants and animals of the world is used throughout his later great works the* Species Plantarum *(1753) and* Systema Naturae *(1758). The purpose of his journey, made at the request of the Swedish parliament, the Riksdag, was chiefly economic. Sweden at that time was a poor country still recovering from the disastrous wars of Charles XII and Linnaeus's instructions concentrated on the agricultural methods, use of plants for food, medicine, dyes, etc.; that is why readers may find curious mentions of lime kilns, crops and cattle. Of course Linnaeus, being at heart a naturalist, was most interested in the natural life. His style is simple and direct; he even apologizes: 'My style of writing is very simple, which will no doubt earn me a low reputation among the nightingales of Pliny.'*

Map of Öland
The old place names from the time of Linnaeus are in brackets next to the new names on this list.

Persnäs (Pesnäs)
Norra Möckleby (Norre Möckleby)
Gårdby (Gårby)
Klinta (Klint)
Smedby (Smeby)
Vickleby (Wickleby)
Blå Jungfrun (Blåkulla)

1 Greater Stitchwort *Stellaria holostea*
2 Bulbous Buttercup *Ranunculus bulbosus*
3 Blackthorn *Prunus spinosa*
4 House Martin *Delichon urbica*
5 Midges (swarming) *Chironomus plumosus*
6 Dor Beetle *Geotrupes stercorarius*

Grankulla
Böda
Blå Jungfrun
Horn
Högby
Gaxa
Persnäs
Köping
Borgholm
Kläppinge
Gärdslösa
Högsrum
Färjestaden
Norra Möckleby
Gårdby
Vickleby
Resmo
Kastlösa
Hulterstad
Smedby
Klinta
Segerstad
Möckleby
Ottenby

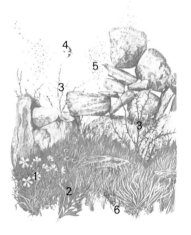

40

An introduction to the Öland journey

The Baltic islands offered a rich and scientifically almost virgin area for investigation; the last thorough survey had been conducted in 1658 by Rudbeck the Elder. So, on 15 May 1741, at the age of thirty-four, accompanied by six student helpers, Linnaeus set off from Stockholm. By 28 May they had reached the port of Kalmar across the sound from Öland. Today a bridge, the longest in Europe, links the island with the mainland; in Linnaeus's time the journey took at least two hours by boat. Öland is a long narrow island consisting largely of an almost flat limestone plateau, the 'alvar'. This alvar karst in some ways resembles the limestone pavements of the Burren district of Ireland, with sunken areas which are covered with water in winter but often dry out during the summer months. The distinctive flora of the island includes a few species not found elsewhere in Sweden; for example Artemisia oelandica, Helianthemum oelandicum, Plantago tenuiflora and Ranunculus illyricus, and many plants found otherwise only on Gotland. The island also has 27 species of wild orchids. On this journey Linnaeus describes a visit to the small island of Blå Jungfrun off the northeast corner of Öland. This interesting place is now a Swedish park and nature reserve. In many parts, the island must have changed drastically since Linnaeus first laid eyes on it, although most of the plants can still be found in the same place. The bridge, a superb example of modern engineering, has made it a very popular holiday place for Swedish people — especially as the island has dry hot summers. This influx of visitors profits the economy of the island, but, together with agricultural activity, puts the wild parts at risk. Fortunately the Swedes protect their wild flowers.

left Blackthorn covered with
lichens, including *Evernia prunustri*

above Öland Spikes *Helmintolithos orthoceratite*

1 June

As soon as we touched the shore of Öland, we realized that this was a land altogether different from the rest of the Swedish provinces. Thus we decided to mark down everything we would see on the island, to the utmost detail.

The blackthorn bushes were made white by a moss [lichen], which almost entirely covered them. *Lichenoides LV Dillenii* [*Evernia prunastri*]. *Alsine foliis lanceolatis serrulatis* [greater stitchwort], which has not been described as a Swedish plant before, was found growing under the junipers.

The wood we first came to was full of birch and juniper, among which grew blackthorn and dog roses, so that only with the greatest difficulty could one get through it. The soil was a deep and beautiful black mould, disturbed everywhere by the swine.

There were many fossils or 'Öland spikes', *Helmintolithus nautili recti* [*orthoceratites*] in the dry stone walls. Also a strangely shaped petrifaction which was common in this place and which we considered to be an impression of *Helmintolithus echini*.

Midges in their thousands, like enormous swarms of bees, flew from the bushes near the shore. Scarabs were rolling in the horse dung; *Hirundo dorso nigro* etc. [house martins] were busy with their nests under the eaves of the local houses.

2 June

We left Färjestaden at 4 o'clock in the morning. The pharmacist from Kalmar, Mr Nordstedt, accompanied us in order to look for medicinal plants. We rode towards Borgholm Castle. The weather was fine, the ground was even, the thrushes sang in the trees. A quarter of a mile from Färjestaden we left the main road towards the left and rode on to a beautiful meadow belonging to the Björnhovda. This district was very pleasant, with many deciduous trees, especially birch and hazel. Here occur the rarest plants, such as have never been heard of in Sweden before, and to see which I travelled in 1738 from Paris to Fontainbleau, where I saw them without thinking I would ever see them again.

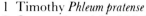

Meadows in flower

The *Cypripedium bulbis subrotundis* etc. [fly orchid] bears such a resemblance to flies that an uneducated person who sees it might well believe that two or three flies were sitting on the stalk. Nature has made a better imitation than any art could ever perform. The magnificent *Orchis bulbis indivisis* etc. [military orchid] has never been seen in Sweden before. The burnt-tip orchid is as unknown in Sweden as the two others. Green-winged orchid was also found.

Elder and wild service tree grew abundantly in the woods, so there is no need for pharmacists to order elder juice from Germany. *Pulsatila flore minore nigricante* [small pasque flower], which I have seen growing wild around Lübeck but never in Sweden, occurred in all dry patches.

3 June

Borgholm Castle is built on a promontory of the alvar on the northwest side of Öland. The castle is of considerable size, rectangular, surrounded by walls. The ground between the castle and its walls is filled up with earth to the

1 Timothy *Phleum pratense*
2 Green-winged Orchid *Orchis morio*
3 Burnt-tip Orchid *Orchis ustulata*
4 Fly Orchid *Ophrys insectifera*, being pollinated by wasp *Gorytes campestris*
5 Flattened Meadow Grass *Poa compressa*

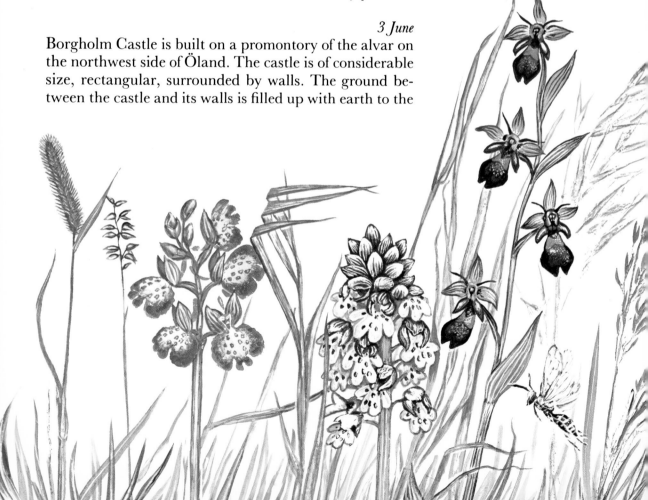

6
7
8
9
10

6 Military Orchid *Orchis militaris*
7 Nodding Melick *Melica nutans*
8 Small Pasque Flower *Pulsatilla pratensis*
9 Common Quaking Grass *Briza media*
10 Meadow Barley *Hordeum secalinum*

height of the wall. There were four round towers, one in each corner.

Here we left the main road for Helvetesgrind (Hell's Gate) still looking unsuccessfully for Linder's violets [sweet violets]; instead we found the *Sanicula* [sanicle] of the pharmacies abundant in the wood beneath the slope. Hazel bushes, very small and hardly 1-2 ells tall but nevertheless with much fruit, grew here at the edge of the alvar.

These small hazel bushes would be excellent for low hedges in gardens, if they would only stay as short as this. However, we noticed that the further down the slope we went, the taller the hazel was, and in the lowland it was like ordinary hazel. This means that its shortness is due to the bedrock and not to its own nature.

A white clay is found in Högsrum's parish near Väster-Sörby, in a bog called Västerkärr; the inhabitants used it to whitewash walls and chimneys. Dye-yielding plants used by the inhabitants of the district are wild marjoram (*Origanum*) for red, bur marigold (*Bidens*) for orange, and buckthorn berries for green.

Mezereon grew in the bogs not far from the church. Late in the evening we went out to listen to the song of the birds called 'kledra' here; they turned out to be nightingales, which delighted us with their lovely singing.

We spent the night at Glömminge.

The region around Borgholm Castle

4 June

Limax cinereus maculatus [*Limax maximus*], a big wood slug, was seen under the trees. It was black with a furrowed back and wavy fragmented ridges, the breast looking like shagreen; it had four small horns and the pore was on the right side of the breast.

All the way from Björnhovda to Torslunda the road passed through delightful groves.

The *Potentilla caule fruticoso* [shrubby cinquefoil] is a bush which is extremely rare in the world, for hitherto botanists have seen it only in York in England and, recently, in Siberia, and now in south Öland. This potentilla grew in tussocks in the alvar. It is as big as lavender, has yellow flowers and sheds the outer bark layer every year. The bush is used for low hedges in gardens where it grows well. The Ölanders make no use of it except to make whisks for scouring kettles from the hard and rigid twigs.

We travelled towards Resmo along the bottom of the slope, which was very steep with bare cliffs on our left and the sea on our right. The road passed through the most lovely groves one could ever hope to see, which for beauty surpassed all other places in Sweden and competed with all in Europe. They consisted of lime, hazel and oak. The ground was smooth and green and there were the most delightful meadows and cornfields. A more pleasant resort cannot be found for anyone who has grown tired of the capriciousness of the world and wishes to retire from its vanity into a quiet obscurity.

We saw several fairy rings in the meadows. All consisted of *Cynosurus bracteis integris* [blue moor-grass]. When this grass grows in a shallow soil, it looks like a blue circle, which common people believe to be caused by fairies dancing. Scientists have attributed it to the nature of the soil, to exhalations, or to horse dung. But here it is quite clear that fairy rings are nothing but this grass, which spreads in all directions and finally withers in the centre, creating a ring.

below Shrubby Cinquefoil
Potentilla fruticosa
bottom Great Grey Slug *Limax maximus*

opposite top Stone circle

opposite below Blue Moor Grass
Sesleria caerulea
opposite bottom Rockrose
Helianthemum oelandicum

The crops are so good here in Resmo that the inhabitants are able to sell grain and buy wooden vessels for household use from the northern parts where there is forest.

Moles are few here, weasels are numerous, and swans are seen only in the spring. The black guillemot is a sea-bird as big as a raven.

The nightingales were singing beautifully in the evening. We stayed the night at Resmo with the rural dean.

5 June

A very big oak tree, which was cut down last winter, had a diameter of 7¼ ells, the bark excluded. As we counted the annual rings, we found it was 260 years old and also noted that some rings in the wood were very close together while others were much further apart. As I considered what had caused this, it occurred to me that cold winters might cause closer rings; thus I counted the rings from the bark towards the centre to the year 1708-1709, the year of the very cold winter, for which I found the rings very close to one another; likewise for the years 1587 and 1658. Thus we have in the oak trunk a chronicle of winters, from which we can tell the weather two to three hundred years back.

47

The Alvar

Cistus Oelandicus Rudbeckii [rockrose; *Helianthemum oelandicum*] was today common on the alvar and differs from *Helianthemum vulgare* in that the flowers are much smaller, the sepals not bent back, the ovary or germen is smooth, the style curved, the stigma rough, four-parted, and the stamens shorter with the anthers light yellow, not dark gold. The petals are narrow and notched. The stalk or scapus is red, straighter and smoother. The flowers are most often closed. With so many differences it is evident that this is distinct from the common *Helianthemum* and is a plant which in Sweden has only been seen on Öland and is rare in all Europe.

Other plants in the alvar deserve attention, since they thrive in the driest and most sterile soil.

We had a keen desire to see an 'alvargrim', a bird said to live only on the alvar and whose name we had not heard before. The gamekeeper whom we sent out caught up with us on the alvar with a shot 'alvargrim'. As soon as I saw it I realized that it was very similar to the golden plover which I had seen before only in the mountains of Lapland. This *Pluvialis* is as big as a dove. Head, neck, back, wings and tail are mottled in white, black and yellow brown. This is because each feather is black with a few yellowish-brown spots on the sides and lighter spots on the tip.

flying, left Lapwing *Vanellus vanellus*
flying, right, and standing Golden
Plover *Pluvialis apricaria*

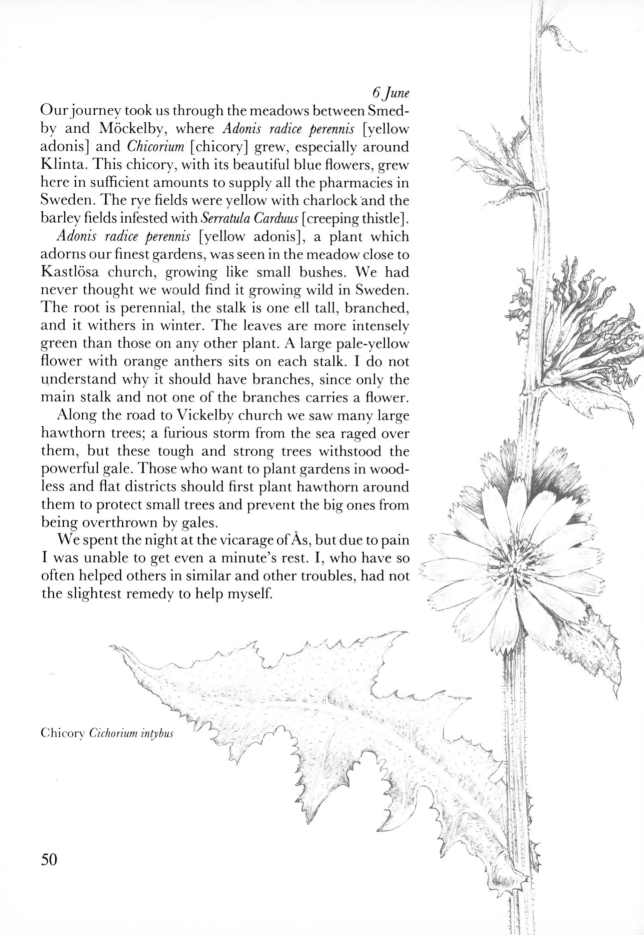

Our journey took us through the meadows between Smed-by and Möckelby, where *Adonis radice perennis* [yellow adonis] and *Chicorium* [chicory] grew, especially around Klinta. This chicory, with its beautiful blue flowers, grew here in sufficient amounts to supply all the pharmacies in Sweden. The rye fields were yellow with charlock and the barley fields infested with *Serratula Carduus* [creeping thistle].

Adonis radice perennis [yellow adonis], a plant which adorns our finest gardens, was seen in the meadow close to Kastlösa church, growing like small bushes. We had never thought we would find it growing wild in Sweden. The root is perennial, the stalk is one ell tall, branched, and it withers in winter. The leaves are more intensely green than those on any other plant. A large pale-yellow flower with orange anthers sits on each stalk. I do not understand why it should have branches, since only the main stalk and not one of the branches carries a flower.

Along the road to Vickelby church we saw many large hawthorn trees; a furious storm from the sea raged over them, but these tough and strong trees withstood the powerful gale. Those who want to plant gardens in wood-less and flat districts should first plant hawthorn around them to protect small trees and prevent the big ones from being overthrown by gales.

We spent the night at the vicarage of Ås, but due to pain I was unable to get even a minute's rest. I, who have so often helped others in similar and other troubles, had not the slightest remedy to help myself.

Chicory *Cichorium intybus*

50

Yellow Adonis *Adonis vernalis*

This day was a Sunday, hence we rested here all day.

It is a custom of the inhabitants of this district to pluck the geese while they are still alive. Nature teaches them to do so, since, when the ducks are sitting on their eggs, they pluck off their own down to cover the eggs and keep them warm while the mother is looking for food. We were told that the feathers were only loosely attached and the geese do not dislike the procedure. Thus, this method should be used all over Sweden since feathers are expensive and indispensible. It should be noted, however, that the people do not pluck all the feathers from the geese; only the down and the small feathers should be plucked where the plumage is densest.

An *Acarus* [mite; *Sericothrombidium holosericeum*] which occurred here was entirely red, with a rather small head, two eyes and eight feet (all these having many joints), a large abdomen, compressed at the head end, raised at the side and with a shaggy velvet-like rear end. It could hardly be differentiated from the water mite, but when put in water it floated and did not know how to dive.

The *Acarus* which is also called *Scorpio araneus* [*Chelifer cancroides*], walked backwards to avoid falling on its nose, despite the large 'hands' it has to break a fall; the foreclaws are like a scorpion's.

Geum rivate [water avens] was found in various places growing in profusion. The corolla had 10-15 petals, few stamens; out of the centre in place of a pistil grew a style, where in a single normal nodding flower would be proper stamens and a pistil.

After church service, a man collected us together to enquire about us and our plans. He took us for spies and said that before the last war three spies had been there, who had been executed at Hulterstad; he had noticed that we observed everything, investigated every situation, and that I had all the time counselled my company with the words that they should have eyes for everything; therefore we were advised to take with us a state attendant, which we did.

51

The southern cape

8 June

We travelled southwards towards the southernmost point of Öland, through the groves and parks of Ottenby.

Midges *Tipula thorace virescente* etc. (*Chironomous plumosus*) were in the wood all along to the sea, in indescribable abundance. They flew into our mouths and faces and we were told that because of them the deer leave the woods for the fields at this time of year.

A dry-stone wall crossed the promontory at the southern border of Ottenby park, separating it from the southernmost flat part of the island. Nearby we saw the ruins of the Rosenkind chapel, which was maintained formerly by the many fishing villages here on the island in the old days when the herring passed these shores annually. Now that these have turned away, both chapel and fishing villages have declined.

Oyster-catchers and lapwings were flying and screeching above us. We shot an oyster-catcher (*Haematopus*) injuring its wing so that it could not fly. The mate flew away, then returned almost immediately, reluctant to forsake the victim. We examined the injured bird; the bill was longer than the head, compressed from the sides, more so from the tip, which was more yellowish, with the upper jaw slightly longer, bright red in colour; there is no other Swedish bird with so red a bill. Two white birds, slightly bigger than seagulls and unknown to us, were seen on land, but they flew up as we approached. One of them was soon shot, and we were told that they are only found at the southern cape of Öland. The mate flew out to sea, where it swam like a duck. The bill is the most remarkable thing about this bird, the avocet (*Recurvirostra* etc.); it is black, bent downwards, three times longer than the head. It is all the more remarkable since it is the only species to which the Creator has given a recurved bill, which it uses like a plough in the mud, to find its food.

Mites are found on most birds and four-footed beasts, and even on fish. The oyster-catcher mite [*Saemundssonia haematopi*] is as big as a flea, hard and tough. It ran fast and

Above: A net for catching seals – sketch from Linnaeus's journals.

1 Spear-leaved Orache *Atriplex hastata*
2 Stinking Chamomile *Anthemis cotula*
3 Sea Milkwort *Glaux maritima*
4 Grass-leaved Orache *Atriplex littoralis*
5 Herring *Clupeus harengus*

was yellow-brown in colour. The avocet mite [*Pediculus recurvirostrae*] was dark and oblong with the head almost triangular and crossed by a furrow.

We saw several lapwings' nests in the fields, mostly with four eggs, which were greyish and unevenly spotted with dark and black dots. In one of the eggs, which we opened and which had lain under the mother for some time, we saw the developing strands of life with many branched blood-red veins, a pale heart and two black eyes.

From here our journey proceeded northwards along the eastern coast of Öland. Although we had never seen it in the wild in Sweden before, a *Euphorbia* called *Tithymalus maximus Oelandicus* [marsh spurge] grew abundantly here in the middle of a field close to a little brook; it grew as shrubs a few ells high. The stem perishes each year; the leaves are alternate, lanceolate and entire.

Small flour mills, which are driven with water in spring and autumn only, were seen along the sides of the alvar. The pond, built of stone and peat, was dry now: there was seaweed stuffed between the stones, a practice which one had not seen in Sweden before, although it is well worth noticing; the seaweed does not rot easily, it swells and is so to say rejuvenated every time it becomes wet and then it is better than anything else for keeping the pond water-tight.

We spend the night at Hulterstad, a quarter of a mile from Segerstad.

Lapwing's nest – usually a pad, constructed from various materials, such as grass, wigs, leaves and mosses, gathered from the surrounding area

9 June

As soon as we got up this morning we walked down to the seashore. The grass was wet with dew and the skylarks chorused in the air.

Cartloads of seaweed (*Fucus*) were taken from the shore to the fields, where it was put into heaps. One man would spread it on the field and another man ploughed it into the soil so that only the tips were seen above the surface to protect the crops when they came forth from the grain. The farmers told us that in sandy fields this seaweed is soon turned into mould, although it is not very rich manure.

All the plants that grow on the seashore turn into succulent types, although the majority of them, when growing in other places have ordinary thin and dry leaves.

Such plants were *Atriplex angustissimo & longissimo folio* [grass-leaved orache], *Plantago latifolia* [ratstail plantain], *Glaux* [sea milkwort] and *Galium luteum* [lady's bedstraw].

Scarabeus niger etc. [beetle; *Carabus nitens*], was running on the beach; when we caught it, it spewed out its poison to avenge itself on us.

Melampyrum spicis conicis laxis laceris [field cow-wheat] grew in the cornfields with purple spikes and a straight stalk, a plant which had previously only been seen growing among the crops.

Norre Möckelby was situated half a mile from Gårdby, but since we saw nothing remarkable, we continued to Runsten church, a half-mile journey.

Ratstail Plantain *Plantago major*
and Ground Beetle *Carabus nitens*

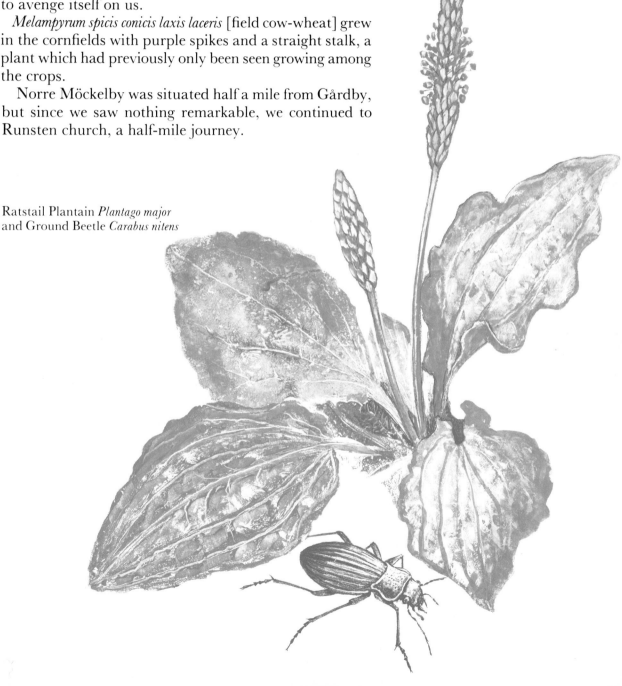

Along the eastern coast

11 June

To the south of Kläppinge chapel we had occasion to see a lump-sucker fish (*Cyclopterus S Lumpus*), which is said to be rarely caught and then only when a storm is approaching. A fish called 'kuder' was mentioned here and in other places, but we had no opportunity to see it; according to the description it was identical to the eelpout of Småland.

Hemp and flax were seen in a few places; these are uncommon here and indeed not common elsewhere. On Lillholmen promontory the land is low and has no hills, the sea wind blows over it continuously and it is thus very suitable for growing woad.

Artemisia foliis compositis etc. [sea wormwood] grew so abundantly on the islet as to colour it all white; it smelled so pleasing and strong. *Cochlearia danica repens* [early scurvy grass] with its pentagonal leaves and smooth pods, grew

quite commonly here on the shore; this plant is so well known for its power against scurvy that there is no need to go into detail.

We found snowdrop wildflower (*Anemone sylvestris*) growing abundantly among the stones at the edges of the cornfields immediately before we came to the village of Husvalla. This pleasing and large flower ought to be generally planted in gardens, especially since it flowers for a long time. This anemone is similar to the wood anemone, but stem, leaves and flowers are three times as big; the wood anemone is glabrous, but in this one the stem, leaf-stalks and the underside of the leaves are bestrewn with white hairs; this flower has five petals, which are ovate and often notched at the end, but the flower of the wood anemone has usually more petals, which are more deeply notched.

The journey continued, we saw many marshes alongside the road; a strong southwest wind blew and rain fell now and then until late in the evening when we reached Södvick inn, where we spent the night, a quarter of a mile from Persnäs.

12 June

The crop grown here is mostly rye; there is little barley since the sandy soil is too hard when there is a drought.

Wild swine are most common in the northern district and do the farmers much harm, since they dig up the ground, like a plough, and trample down the crops; they walk about and beat the crops together like sheaves, so that they can fill their mouths with ears of corn at each bite. Sometimes they mate with the domesticated swine, which produce wilder offspring.

Campanula hispida etc. [bell flower; *Campanula cervicaria*], which is very rare in the rest of Sweden, was common in the meadows here; the stem was fairly tall, without branches, unevenly pentagonal and bestrewn with transparent reflexed bristles; the leaves had wavy margins.

Asperula Rubia Cyanchica dicta [bedstraw; *Galium triandrum*] grew abundantly in the meadows; it has red bushy roots, which should be tried for dyeing, since the plant is closely related to *Galium album* [northern bedstraw].

We did not see any particularly interesting insects today; only the aphis *Aphis cirsii*, dark, with six rows of elevated spots along the back; the wing buds, the feet and the true horns black; the thighs white towards the base.

There was a garden at the vicarage here. When we asked why gardens were so rare on Öland, the answer was that deer enter the gardens during the winter, when the snow cover is higher than the walls, and eat the trees, which are also damaged by the hares.

We stayed at Persnäs during the night.

left Rye *Secale cereale*; Wireworms, the eruciform larvae of the Click Beetle *Agriotes lineatus* and a serious agricultural pest

We left in the morning in the direction of Gaxa, where the main road ends.

Grass worms were seen moving in flocks in the meadows, destroying the crop; each grub (*Eruca*) was about a finger long, had 16 feet, and the entire body was covered with yellow hair. We threw it to the hens, but they did not dare to try this new food.

below Cinnabar Moth *Hipocrita jacobaeae* and its caterpillar feeding on Groundsel *Senecio vulgaris*

The journey took us through a young oak wood, with hazel and beautiful grass at Långrum village. Twenty pairs of young oaks were planted along the two sides of the road like an alley; they were protected from cattle by poles as high as a man and bound together.

We reached Gaxa at noon; white sand thrown up by the sea lay on the shore in great quantities. At the water's edge the seaweed was packed together, and sand was thrown up on it, forming banks and islets. This is surely the way in which nature has gradually built all the land here.

We have never before seen the seaweed that botanists call *Fucus dichotomus ramosissimus* etc. [*Furcellaria fastigiata*]. It is no thicker than a thread, rounded and densely branched and bifurcated, and all the branches were of equal length, which made it look as if it were cut off at the top.

Potentilla [silverweed] grew directly in the sand and *Senecio minor vulgaris* [groundsel] on the rotting seaweed.

Phalaena seticornis spirilinguis etc. [cinnabar moth; *Hipocrita jacobeae*], a beautiful creature, flew everywhere on the shore; its caterpillar grazes on the groundsel. The body was black, the antennae bristle-like, and it had two little spiralled tongues; the upper wing had a red longitudinal line along the front edge, and at the point and the back edge there was a red spot.

Cicindela viridi-aenea etc. [*Elaphrus riparius*], a little bright-green insect with a copper hue jumped rapidly on the shore. Head, breast, abdomen and feet glittered like copper or gold; the neck was thin and the dark eyes protruded from the skull. The wing cases were green with a copper tinge and had large hollowed-out dots inside them.

The day was calm and nice; the clouds formed rounded landscapes on the horizon after sunset.

We remained in Gaxa during the night to wait for the ship.

Blå Jungfrun, island of the Blue Virgin

Immediately after noon, we hurried to the shore and steered a boat towards Blå Jungfrun, a rock two miles away, all blue and like a hemisphere rising out of the water. A northern wind started to blow and to heave up the waves, and a violent storm shook the boat; we all had to work hard with danger to our lives; and we finally arrived, dead tired.

Blå Jungfrun is a little island situated between the northern point of Öland and Småland. The people say that all the witches have to come here (a troublesome journey indeed) each Maunday Thursday. If any place in the world looks dreadful, this is it, and the description will be appropriately short. It has a rock wall and within this a low deciduous forest of oak, birch, etc.; then rock again, more low woodland, still higher rocks, with the highest in the centre; the rock consists of a red spar-like stone overgrown with patches of pitch-black *Lichenoides* [lichen; *Parmelia dentata*], which, together with the haze, causes the blue colour of Blå Jungfrun. The thicket was so dense that a man could hardly penetrate it and what was remarkable was that the shrubs were also entwined with ivy, which grew all over the place like peas and bindweed. There were deep crevices and channels hewn out of the rock and ground by the sea, and even in the highest rocks there were marks, like waves, as a sign that the sea had raged here too in former times.

We left Blå Jungfrun in the afternoon, wind and waves propelling our boat; Blå Jungfrun lay between the sun and our little ship.

We came onshore at 10.30 pm and rode back to Gaxa immediately.

1 Windswept Scots Pine *Pinus sylvestris*
2 Birch – named by Linnaeus on his island visit *Betula verrucosa*
3 Pedunculate Oak *Quercus robur*
4 Rowan (in shrub form) *Scorbus aucuparia*
5 Ivy *Hedera helix*
6 Common Solomon's Seal *Polygonatum multiflorum*
7 Aspen *Populus tremula*
8 Lichen *Xanthoria parietina*
9 Reindeer Moss *Cladonia rangiferina*

The northern cape

We left Gaxa and Högby church towards Böda and so further to the east side of Öland. The road passed through woods of oak and hazel alternating with spruce. From Böda we proceeded northwards, since we wanted to see the northernmost point of Öland.

The wood consisted of fir, spruce and juniper; the fir trees, which are good for timber, lift their branches towards the sun; the spruce twigs droop and the junipers are bushy. Reindeer moss covered the higher spots. Bilberries, cowberries and heather coloured the ground green. My flower, twinflower (*Linnaea borealis*), with its pairs of drooping flowers, grew in the deep forest and indicated that the place has not been burnt in living memory. *Trientalis* [chickweed wintergreen] grew on the slopes, the flowers bent down to the earth since it had been raining all day. The bog rosemary was in flower in the marshy places and also bracken (*Pteris*) here and there between the glades.

Sjötorp, a farm a mile from Böda, was the end point of today's journey over sand to a beautiful black soil; the farm was enclosed within high fences as protection against the deer. Here we were allowed to shelter from rain and darkness.

18 June

From Sjötorp we proceeded to the next hamlet, Grankulla. Marram grass grew in tussocks on the sand dunes and prevented the sand from blowing away; we tried to dig up the roots but they went down so deep that we could not find the bottom, and were as thick as binding twine, with innumerable ramifications. *Carex spica composita* etc. [sand sedge] grows under the sand with creeping roots; it puts forth little tufts of stalks and leaves evenly spaced at a quarter of an ell apart as if it were planted along a string.

Iberis foliis sinuatis etc. [shepherd's cress] grew in the forests on the sand drifts.

We left the sandhills and proceeded westwards to the bay. *Jasione* [sheepsbit] and *Spergula* [corn spurrey] grew

62

left, top to bottom Juniper *Juniperus communis*; Bracken *Pteridium aquilinum*

below, top to bottom Chickweed Wintergreen *Trientalis europaea*; Shepherd's Cress *Teesdalia nudicaulis*; Narrow-leaved Helleborine *Cephalanthera longifolia*

in the sandy field which had to lie fallow for four or five years after one year's cultivation. On the road we saw tar being distilled and lime was burnt at the bay.

Our way went from Öland's northern cape towards the south, for we followed the western shore as we had already followed the eastern. A hare danced in front of us along the shore.

Woad (*Isatis s. Glastum*) grew wild here upon the shore. The root is thin and survives only two years; it does not come into flower the first year; the root leaves are ovate, narrower at the base, with crenate edges, smooth and not rough. The stem is half to one ell tall. The inflorescence has flowers with yellow spreading petals. The fruits are pendulous. When this plant is chewed, it tastes of kale at first, then has a sharp taste like cress. From this plant people make a blue dye.

Serapis radicibus fibrosis etc. [narrow-leaved helleborine], a plant which we had never seen before, occurred in the wild forest. The road to Torp through the forest showed us a large number of the *Sanicula* [sanicle] of the apothecaries and *Pyrola scapo uniflora* [one-flowered wintergreen] was in full flower.

Wild apple-trees grow all over Böda parish and bear many apples, but the farmers know of no use for them except at the autumn slaughter, when a few apples are added to the meat soup. From these one could, as peasants do in England and Normandy, press out that beautiful cider or apple juice that often competes with wine in flavour and is much more pleasant than the seawater with which we saw the workers in the quarries quench their thirst.

The wild service trees [Swedish whitebeam] were in full flower, the sorb-apples are eaten in the autumn, after the first frost; if they are eaten earlier, they are roasted first.

We could not get any food during the whole day; last year's harvest had been poor and the farmers did not have any bread for their own use; some had not had any for a month, others not for half a year; but after much persuasion we had a drink of milk, nothing else.

We lodged in Byrum, where we were plagued by mosquitos the whole night, as if we had been in Lapland.

Sea holly and ant lions

19 June

Today we spent the time on the sandhills which we left in the late evening yesterday.

'Sandpill' (*Formica-leo*) [ant lion] is the name of an insect which few people in Sweden have seen; we amused ourselves with it. On the smooth surface of the sandhills there were tracks, as if the thong of a whip had been loosely drawn over the sand, and at the end of the track there was a pit, like the impression of the narrow end of an egg in the sand. When we explored these pits, we found the insect between the humid and the dry layers of the sand. It was as big as a spider, grey, with large oval belly. The neck was slender and at the mouth were two claws slightly curved at the tip. These ant lions are the larvae of the 'fly' *Hemerobius* [*Myrmelion formica-leo*] which lays its eggs in the sand, usually in the vicinity of an ant-hill. When the eggs hatch, the larva burrows its way down into the sand until it has made a pit and then waits at the centre. When the ants walk about performing their various tasks, they sometimes reach the brink of the pit and fall down helplessly and are attacked and devoured by the ant lion. When we put an ant in the pit to observe all exactly, we noticed that when the ant was struggling to get out, the ant lion would throw sand at it, so that it slipped and fell into the lion's claws.

Eryngium foliis radicalibus etc. [sea holly] grew here on the shore; it has not been described in Sweden before. The roots go deep into the sand, and the shoots that have not yet reached the surface are white and stout like asparagus and taste good even when raw. The spears of this plant, cooked and eaten like ordinary asparagus, are a delicacy; they are diuretic, purify the blood and raise the spirits.

We found a dead scarab beetle on the shore *Scarabaeus maxillis lunulatis* etc. [*Scarabeus tridentatus*]. The head, the neck and the belly were dark brown, with little excavated spots. The breast was hairy below and prickly on the sides. The creature was as big as a stag beetle but more rounded.

Ant Lion *Myrmeleon formicarius* with (*left*) larva exposed in its excavated pit and (*right*) adult flying
Wood Ant workers *Formica rufa*

Sea Holly *Eryngium maritimum*

Grass Snake *Natrix natrix*

Leaving Öland

Papilio apiformis etc. [*Aegeria apiformis*] was found here on the trees; it was like a bee in shape and size; the wings were white with black veins, the fore-wings were black in the middle as well as at the tips. The antennae were likewise black, but stouter and white in the middle; the abdomen was black with two pale-yellow stripes and a pale-yellow belt and more hirsute and rust-coloured at the tip.

On reaching Byrum we were taken by Superintendant Sahlsten to Horn. On our behalf he contracted with some farmers to ship us to Gotland by the first favourable wind.

20 June

While we were resting and waiting for better weather in Horn, we spent the time looking for plants, insects and other less well known Swedish animals. The strange insect *Curcilio niger* etc. [*Apodectus coryli*] had red densely spotted wing-cases; the breast was red, smooth and narrow. The head looked like a dog's head with a short snout; the eyes protruded.

66

A grass snake was killed; it had a grey back and a black belly; a row of white scales lay along each side of the body; under the chin and throat it was whitish, and on the white upper jaw at the ears light yellow with transverse black lines. All teeth were of equal size, hence the snake is not dangerous.

Draba foliis caulinis etc. [twisted whitlow-grass] grew in the field. The flower spike is tall and the pods egg-shaped and compressed, with the septum between the chambers as broad as the outer wall.

Seals were caught in the parishes of Högby and Böda by means of seal stones and upright or horizontal nets made of horsehair.

21 June

We set sail at 9 o'clock in the evening, after waiting only a couple of hours for a fair wind. The southwesterly carried our ship from the land, which disappeared from our view at the same time as the sun, and our eyes were closed by sleep.

Common Seal *Phoca vitulina*

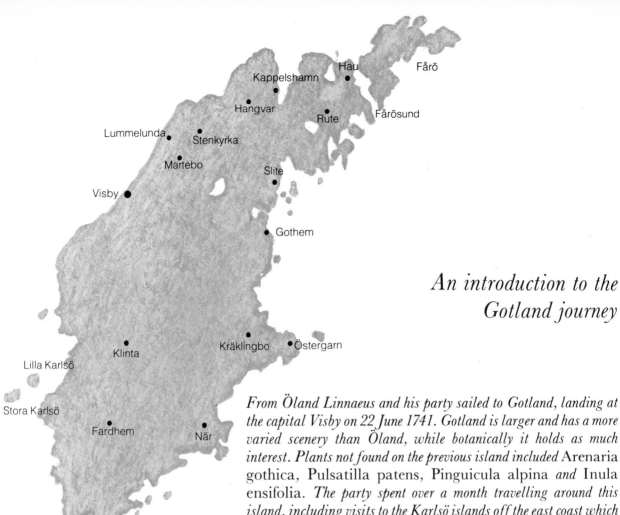

Fårö

Hau

Kappelshamn

Hangvar

Rute

Fårösund

Lummelunda

Stenkyrka

Martebo

Slite

Visby

Gothem

Kräklingbo   •Östergarn

Klinta

Lilla Karlsö

Stora Karlsö

Fardhem

När

Fide

Öja

Hamra

Hoburgen

An introduction to the Gotland journey

From Öland Linnaeus and his party sailed to Gotland, landing at the capital Visby on 22 June 1741. Gotland is larger and has a more varied scenery than Öland, while botanically it holds as much interest. Plants not found on the previous island included Arenaria gothica, Pulsatilla patens, Pinguicula alpina *and* Inula ensifolia. *The party spent over a month travelling around this island, including visits to the Karlsö islands off the east coast which are today famous for their seabird colonies. It was on the smaller of the two islands that Linnaeus discovered one of the rarest of Swedish plants,* Lactuca quercina. *Other rarities included* Artemesia rupestris *and* Gypsophilia fastigata.

Map of Gotland
The old place-names from the time of Linnaeus are in brackets next to the new names on this list.

Visby (Wisby)
Lummelunda (Lummelund)
Ire (Ihre)
Kappelshamn (Capelhamn)
Rute (Ruthe)
Fårön (Fåröen)
Gothem (Gothum)
Kräklingbo (Krklingebo)
Hamra (Hambre)
Fardhem (Fardum)
Stora Karlsö (Stora Carlsö)
Lilla Karlsö (Lilla Carlsö)
Klinta (Klint)

Visby city wall with (*bottom left*)
Viper's Bugloss *Echium vulgare* and
(*to its right*) Swine's Succory
Arnoseris minima

We awoke at dawn, 2 o'clock in the morning, and found the Karlsö islands before our eyes. The wind died down gradually, the ship glided on; the sides of the islands appeared more and more steep and high, like fortress walls. The sea grew calm and smooth as a mirror, on which velvet scoters swam here and there; no porpoises were seen, nor any ships.

Klinteberg came nearer and Gotland's shore lay on our right hand, while the Karlsö islands were left behind. The sun shone warmly; time passed till 2 o'clock in the afternoon, when we landed at Visby.

Visby is the only town in Gotland and is situated midway along the west coast. The town seemed to us like a model of Rome. So many, so large and such splendid churches stood all over the town, now roofless and turned into ruins by the changing times. The inhabitants were good-humoured, polite and friendly; their speech was somewhat different from ordinary Swedish and was like Norwegian in accent.

There were several uncommon plants on streets and in churchyards. For example: *Echium* [viper's bugloss], *Conium* [hemlock], *Chenopodium 2: dum* [upright goosefoot], *Chaerophyllum caule maclato* etc. [rough chervil], *Hyoseris caule diviso nudo* etc. (swine's succory), *Scandix seminibus* etc., or true chervil, which has never been seen in Sweden, grew wild among the crops; but anybody collecting chervil for domestic use should beware of *Aethusa* [fool's parsley] if he would keep his sanity, since both plants grow together and are quite similar.

25 June

Although we had ordered horses yesterday in order to leave early in the morning, we did not get any until the afternoon; however we spent the time describing some sea-birds.

Red-breasted merganser. The bill is rounded with backwards-pointing sharp 'teeth'; the upper jaw is prolonged at the tip; head bluish-black with a long hanging crest. Throat whitish, breast yellow in front. Feet and bill red.

Anas rostri extremo dilatato etc. [shoveler duck]. The bill is rather broad and rounded at the end, with a hooked tip, and teeth like small scales.

The *Larus* [common gull] is as big as a hen and all white except for the wings and back, which are light grey.

We took our course from Visby northwards along the west coast. Daisies, which are used in pharmacies and which I have hitherto seen only on the plains of Skåne, grew here abundantly.

left to right Hemlock *Conium maculatum*; Rough Chervil *Chaerophyllum temulentum*; Fool's Parsley *Aethusa cynapium*

The pastures were covered with bearberries, cowberries, rockrose, juniper and pine. Many fields were yellow with charlock and the meadows were yellow with meadow buttercup. *Cotoneaster* [great orme berry] and sheepsbit grew on the hills.

71

Martebo Church

One and three-quarter miles from the town we passed Lummelunda church and not far from here we found a plant, growing abundantly, which has never before been discovered in Sweden. Ramsons was the name of the plant, which here grew under the bushes; the root was an oblong bulb surrounded by bristles. The leaves were lanceolate and in shape similar to the lily of the valley. The farmers say that where this plant grows, it drives away other herbs and weeds; they plant it among the hops to keep wild chervil and other weeds away. The cattle eat it willingly, but it gives a garlic taste to milk and butter.

Sedge grew in the marshes near the church. People use this tall grass to thatch most of their farmyard roofs; it is mown with a scythe between midsummer and the feast of St Olaf and is bundled while still fresh, without regard to which end is up or down; roofs thatched with this are better and tighter than those covered with straw. By the sedge grew an orchid we had not seen before – the *Orchis morio mas* [early purple orchid]. The farmers here call all orchids 'St John's keys'.

·In the morning we went out to botanize in Martebo. In the fields and on the roads grew *Anagallis flore rubro* [scarlet pimpernel]. Also by the wayside *Ophioglossum* [adder's tongue fern], from which a healing ointment was made. *Geum floribus nuntantibus* [water avens] was here called 'catballs' and cornflowers 'sailors' hats' because of the colour and structure of the flowers.

Household remedies were:
The *Valerianae radix* [root of common valerian] for hysteria; for the ague, gunpowder, strong liquor, snuff and tobacco as an emetic; for stitch, *Semina Cardui Mariae* [fruits of the milk thistle].

Yellow colouring is here got from buckthorn (*Rhamnus catharticus*) and alder buckthorn (*Frangula*), of which the dried bark is boiled after being steeped in weak lye or a mixture of lye and water.

Maypoles were erected by the farm girls in the church as midsummer decoration; they were beautifully covered with flowers of several kinds and chips of horn, snow white as fresh parchment.

left to right Ramsoms *Allium ursinum*; Water Avens *Geum rivale*; Early Purple Orchid *Orchis mascula*; Sedge *Cladium mariscus*

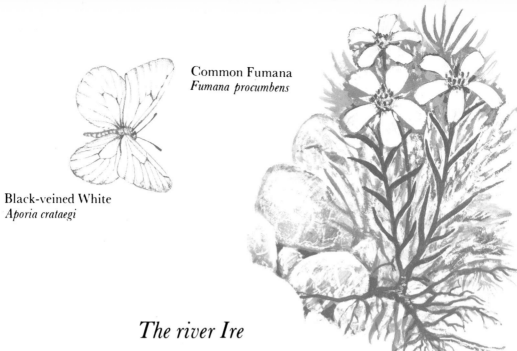

Common Fumana
Fumana procumbens

Black-veined White
Aporia crataegi

The river Ire

Reflexed Stonecrop *Sedum reflexum*

Wall-rue Fern *Asplenium rutamuraria*

Stenkyrka did not show us anything remarkable, but after a further journey of a quarter of a mile, we found on the lefthand side a limestone rock where we discovered some plants which have hardly ever been seen in Sweden.

Cistus caule procumbente etc. [common fumana] grew here on the limestone rock; I have only seen it before at Fontainbleau in France. It is easily distinguished from other kinds of *Cistus* as the leaves are not paired but scattered. We did not find it anywhere else. *Sedum foliis sublatis* etc. [rock stonecrop] and *Ruta-muraria* [wall rue (fern)] used in pharmacies and hitherto imported from abroad grew on these bald rocks.

Bladder sedge with its long beautiful leaves, was seen growing in bundles; it should be planted in marshes, for no other grass grows more luxuriously; below the male spikes, which terminate the stem, one very often found some female flowers.

Further along, the river Ire passed under our limestone road, and we found several natural history specimens in it. Water beetles and *Nepae abdominis margine integro* were moving under the surface. *Hirudo octoculata* [*Nephelis octoculata*] a white oval leech, was found under the stones in the water; it is often found very large in the stomachs of

74

small fishes, and I would believe that the worms found in the livers of sheep are nothing but the spawn of this leech, since the sheep pick up these worms while grazing in marshy places.

Phryganae were lying on the bottom of the stream, rolling in their cylindrical tubes made out of sand.

The *Papilo hexapus* etc. [black-veined white butterfly] was also found here. We have seen bearberry more plentifully in every bare patch of the forest today than in any other place, so that, should anyone desire it in great quantities, he could not get it more easily than in these districts.

This hot day ended with the sun setting in a wall of clouds. After a journey of one and three-quarter miles, we had to lodge for the night near Hangvar church.

27 June

Leech *Nephelis octoculata*

At 4 o'clock in the morning we rose to read four runic stones lying close to each other in Hangvar churchyard. *Lichen crustaceus candidus* etc. [*Lecanora calcarea*], a white lichen that hindered so much of our reading of runic stones on Öland, was noted to grow predominantly on limestone, which made it possible to distinguish limestone from granite at a great distance.

Water Scorpion *Nepa cinerea*
Caddis Fly *Phryganea grandis* —
larvae in their cases

Flounders and the coral shore

Seals are caught on the coast mainly in two ways: with 'lying nets' and 'standing nets'. Seal stones are big stones lying close to the water line, a little above the surface, smooth and large; where there are no stones, they are put there by the farmers. The standing nets are placed in a half circle around the seal stone, for if the seal is going to rest or sleep, it has to find such a stone, upon which it always climbs from the landward side and rests upon it with its nose towards the sea; when the seal is frightened, it quickly makes for the sea and is caught in the net.

Flounders are caught in some quantity with fishing tackle baited with cut pieces of herring. We noticed that these flounders were of two kinds: the larger [turbot] has eyes on the left side, which is rough, grey and without red spots. The smaller [flounder] has eyes on the right side, which is grey with flame-coloured spots.

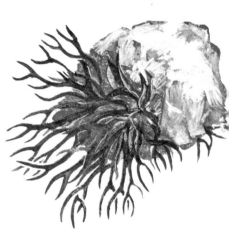

left Seaweed *Furcellaria fastigiata*
below left Flounder *Platichthys flesus*
below Sea Campion *Silene maritima*

I call the shore that lies to the eastern side of Kappelshamn 'coral shore'. It was very broad and covered with white and grey stones; this greatly surprised us, since each one stone was nothing but a coral, called *Madrepora*, so that anyone who wants to collect exquisite corals need try no other place than this; every man in the world could probably get a cartload of his own corals here. The beach was undulating like a ploughed field, with ridges parallel to the water, gradually increasing in height towards the land; all were quite bare and consisted of coral rubble stones. The *Madreporae* lying close to the water were clean and clear, adorned with stars like the backs of playing cards or the cells of a honeycomb. All these coral stones are, according to the findings of the learned botanist Bernard Jussieu, nothing but the shells of small worms, who make the stars and stone crusts, and there are many species of these worms.

Lepidium foliis pinatis etc. [hutchinsia] was growing on the coral shore, together with *Cucubalus* etc. [sea campion], which grew in the coral ridges.

Prunella [self-heal] was growing here too, with such extraordinary flowers that at first we thought we had discovered a new species; but we soon found it was only a variety (probably *P. grandiflora*).

I must say that Hau was the finest farm I saw in the whole country; on two sides it borders on the sea and a little lake, and on the other two it is surrounded by vast sterile limestone rocks. Two tenant farmers lived here; each of them had his own white and beautiful stone house, with a farmstead of tarred wood. Everything inside the house was clean and proper; the kitchen was full of copper kettles, large and small, ten to fifteen in each place. The farmsteads were surrounded by hop yards and gardens and huge leafy maple trees on which there were several small, hollow wooden cylinders, wherein starlings and other small birds could lay their eggs and delight the inhabitants with continuous music. There were also beautiful wood piles to enclose the yard further. Here one felt the truth of the well-known words: 'A farmer with eight cows and a horse, who lives in the forest, free from many a guest, he of all lives best.'

We spent the night here at Hau.

Fårö

After a mile we reached Rute church, where we botanized. During our 'inquisition' of the pastures, we collected the following plants: *Gentiana corolla hypocrateriformi* [field gentian; *Gentianella campestris*], *Astragalus Rivini* [wild liquorice], *Campanula caule angulato* [clustered bellflower].

We passed Bunge church and continued onwards towards Fårö. Fårö sound, which separates Fårö from the rest of Gotland, is about an eighth of a mile broad. We took the ferry boat across. The eider duck is common on the islets, but not rightly treated on the islands; the birds are shot and, what is still worse, their eggs are used for making pancakes. Indeed, throughout the spring one can see these birds decorating the fish market in Stockholm. The time will probably come when the excellent down of these birds will save them from being shot.

above Clustered Bellflower *Campanula glomerata*
below Field Gentian *Gentianella campestris*
right Marram Grass *Ammophila arenaria*

Early in the morning we left Fårö church and rode along the eastern shore towards the northernmost point of Fårö.

Four kinds of seaweed were used as manure: 'Ylle', 'krakel', 'tang' and 'hauter'. 'Ylle' (*Conferva marina ramosissima*) [*Pilayella littoralis*] is the best manure, but when too much of it is spread on the field it does it harm. 'Krakel' (*Fucus dichotomus ramosissimus* etc.) [*Furcellaria fastigiata*] is of moderate use, and 'tang' (*Alga angstifolia Vitrarium I.B.*) [eelgrass] the least useful. 'Hauter' (*Fucus folio dichotomo integro*) [bladder wrack; *Fucus vesiculosus*] is especially good after it has been heaped and become well rotted. We saw huge stacks of it, in which the cattle were prodding about, doubtless to lick the salt.

Dunes of shifting sands lay here and there at the shore, thrown up by the sea; but at the northernmost point the whole land was covered with this sand, which formed high and uneven sand-hills. This reminded us of the Dutch dunes. The sand in these dunes was fine, white and clear. The irregularities in the sand hillocks were caused by

marram grass, which grew everywhere here among the sand hillocks. It is a strange grass, which in the driest sand grows rampantly both high and tall, and the further it comes up in the sand, the more runners branch off, one from each joint. The leaves under the sand wither and become dry; this makes the lower part of the plant look like a broom, from which the sand cannot escape. We dug to try and find the grass's lowermost root, but we could not dig deep enough in the loose sand; we noticed, though, that the grass grows not only straight up in the sand but also sideways. The use of the grass is varied, since where it grows the shifting sands cast up by the sea are retained on the shore and cannot drift inland and cause harm; the more sand that drifts on the grass, the better it grows and the higher the hill becomes. The marram grass with its sand hills prevents the land from flooding in winter; in Holland one can see how the dunes between Haarlem and the Hague form a barrier that shuts out water from the low-lying Netherlands.

On the beach ran in great abundance the insect *Carabus nigricans* etc. [beetle; *Bembidium velox*]; it was so agile that, although it had shells on its wings, it was swifter in flight than any bee; it was completely black, as big as a housefly and the wing shells were grooved with eight fine lines; the breast-shield was smooth and the antennae half as long as the body.

The most northerly point of Fårö had nothing remarkable about it but a flat sandy beach on which the sea had sketched several mountains and high alps as with a pen.

Ducks in millions, all quite grey, were swimming in the water and flying about us. The many seabirds that hatch their eggs in Sweden leave here for the most part uninjured, but they are caught in Holland and other southern countries, and the market places are crowded with them; our nation has not reached such perfection in bird-catching.

The language here on Fårö is somewhat more difficult to understand than that of the rest of Gotland; the farmers talk in a broad dialect and change their vowels into diphthongs, such as 'jau' for 'ja' (yes) and 'naj' for 'nej' (no). They also have many words altogether different from ordinary Swedish.

We lodged the night at Fårö church.

Stone Giants

We crossed over the sound once more at the same place.
Here at Fårö sound the folk were having a feast, which
included dancing by the farmers and their womenfolk.
The measure of the dance was very strange. We were
regaled with 'lura', a drink that is opaque, like the colour
of white wax, and boiled by dropping in glowing stones.
The drink had been brought by a man from Ösel, who was
also playing a bagpipe for the guests.

The bagpipe was remarkable in that it had no seams; it
was made from the whole stomach of a seal; the modulator
was placed in the pylorus and the base, which was hanging down, was inserted into the oesophagus.

Smoke-pits for smoking flounder and herring were built
into the earth and sealed so tight that the smoke could not
escape; they were black on the inside. The fish were hung
up and smoked with fir and pine cones or even rotten oak
or decayed pine stubs as fuel – anything that would burn
without a flame. The smoking lasted four to five hours
only, so that the fish would not become too dry.

1 July

We visited Furilen, the island near Kyllaj, early in the
morning, but it had been grazed and there was nothing
remarkable to see.

A female velvet scoter was shot; it was slightly bigger
than a duck; the bill was similar to that of a goose, dark at
the edge, with many teeth, like upright scales.

Aranea abdomine antice etc. [spider; *Aranea angulata*], a
rather big spider, was found in the trees; the abdomen
went from the breast into an obtuse angle and was vari-
egated with multi-coloured white, yellow and black, but
the legs were only white and black.

Klasen is the name of another island, not far from
Kyllaj; this island is rather long but not very broad. All of
it is pasture. Here grew *Scirpus culmo triquetro* etc. [sea club
rush], *Draba alpina hirsuta Celsii* [twisted whitlow grass],

Rhinanthus etc. [yellow rattle] and *Melilotus officinarium* [tall melilot].

Where the sea had thrown sand and gravel together, woad grew like a field of hemp, and it could be no more luxuriant in a garden. It would be well worth while to sow this dye plant all over the island, since it grows so well here.

Scabiosa corollulis quinquefidis etc. [small scabious], a rare plant that grows wild in Germany and sometimes adorns our gardens, but has never been found wild in Sweden, was growing on the slopes of Klasen.

Birds such as oyster-catchers, gulls and small waders started to worry us and to fly around our heads with intolerable screeches, so that we heard nothing else after we had gone ashore. We shot a wader, a bird that we did not know in appearance, flight or call. This bird, the turnstone (*Tringa nigro* etc.), was like a lapwing, but not bigger than a thrush; abdomen, breast, tail and wings on the underside were white; the head was white above with small yellow-brown spots.

We called what we saw by the sea near Kyllaj the 'Stone Giants'. They were limestone rocks 4-6 fathoms high arranged in a row like the ruins of churches or castles. Those standing at a lower level of the slope were taller than those higher up, so that the heads were all at the same level. From a distance they looked like statues, horses, torsos, and I do not know what kind of ghosts. Evidently this had been formerly a limestone mountain the roots of which had been ground, cut and formed by the heaving waves of the sea. Stone giants of the same size were seen all the way along the road to Slite.

Slite, one of the finest harbours on Gotland, provided us with a night's lodgings.

top Two Great Black-backed Gulls
Larus marinus
below Three Oystercatchers
Haemotopus ostralegus
bottom left Velvet Scoter *Melanitta fusca*
bottom right Turnstone *Arenaria interpres*

81

Dye-yielding plants

Gothem was reached after a one-and-a-quarter-mile journey. The church was beautiful. The goats were left in the open winter and summer, and get no more from the farmer than what they steal from him.

Squirrels have been seen to sail over the lakes on chips of wood or bark according to the people here, and they are supposed to disappear every seventh year. Thereafter, missed very much, they then increase in numbers until the seventh year comes again. This tale is quite new to me, and should be investigated. Weasels are also found here.

Yew trees grew as big as firs or oaks, mostly in the marshlands. The inhabitants had a nice manner of covering their walls with yew twigs, starting from the floor and covering all the wall as with shingles, for which the soft needles made a delightful green wall cover. If Pliny had been invited into such a house, he would never have dared to sleep there one single night or to eat any food, since he believed that to sleep or eat under a yew tree was fatal; this makes people laugh here in Gothem.

Darnel (*Lolium spicis aristatis* etc.) was growing abundantly here and in many places among the barley. Those who drank beer brewed from darnel-mixed barley became mad and almost blind. The farmers thought that if they rubbed their wrists and fingers with the beer, it would protect them from the affliction.

The dye-plants used here in the parish are as follows: Bright yellow is dyed by means of 'flowers of St John' *Flores Buphthalmi* [yellow chamomile flowers]. The yarn is first boiled with a little alum in a copper kettle, then it is dried; after that the dry flowers are boiled for a long time in water and finally the mordanted yarn is added to the decoction.

left to right Yellow Chamomile
Anthemis tinctoria; Saw-wort
Serratula tinctoria; Darnel *Lolium
temulentum*; Woad *Isatis tinctoria*

82

Greenish yellow is dyed with birch leaves boiled in water after mordanting with alum.

Green is dyed thus: first the yarn is dyed yellow with saw-wort (*Serratula*) and then blue with Indigo, since yellow and blue together make green.

Sea-green is dyed with diluted acetic acid and salt in an untinned copper kettle left till it has become verdigrised. Then the yarn is put into it and stirred often to make it evenly dyed, but it is not boiled.

We had to spend the night at Gothem since neither we nor the sheriff had succeeded in obtaining horses, although we had asked for them at noon.

3 July

Torsburgen, the only mountain in the district, was situated just over an eighth of a mile from Kråklingbo; it was a big, high, steep, bare and harsh mountain, flat on the top.

From the top of Torsburgen, the tallest forest looked like a flat field and one could easily count 30 church towers.

Geranium pedunculis bifloris etc. [shining cranesbill], a beautiful herb not hitherto found in Sweden, grew especially on the northern side in the shade among fallen rocks. The root dies after a year; the stalk (and leaves, especially the underside), red, smooth and glossy. The leaves are kidney-shaped, glossy, provided with a stalk, five-lobed, and each lobe three-lobed. The flower stalk has two flowers. The calyx is somewhat swollen, glossy, with five leaves but three-angled, and each angle marked with three raised lines. The petals are entirely flesh-coloured.

Coronilla corollarum etc. [scorpion senna], hitherto seen growing wild only at Vienna, Geneva and Montpellier grew wild here, exposed to the cold north side of Tors-burgen. I would never have believed that this shrub would grow wild in Sweden, even if twenty botanists had said so, had I not seen it for myself.

Papilio hexapus etc. [apollo; *Parnassius apollo*], a large and beautiful butterfly which is not common in Sweden and is very rare abroad, had settled in great numbers in the field on top of the mountain, as if very tired and unable to fly away. The tail had four sharp, hard claws, almost like the claws of a cat, spreading out a little with a pointed style between them.

We spent the night at Östergarn.

Östergarn meadows

The church at Östergarn is situated on the east shore, in the centre of Gotland, where the land is broadest; from here to Västergarn the land is 5 miles wide and from the north cape of Gotland to the south cape it is 15 miles long.

The mountain near the church is high and steep on all sides, as if it were a son of Torsburgen. From the top of the mountain there is a delightful view of the northeast; one saw from here the church at the foot of the mountain, then the beautiful fields and meadows, the green woods, other steep smaller mountains, bays of the sea and blue sea as far as to St Olofsholm, so that it would hardly be possible to find a more lovely place for a summer house anywhere on this island.

Sanguisorba spicis ovatis [great burnet] grew here in the meadows between the sea and the church. The spikes were rounded or oval, bright red on the petals, stamens and pistils.

The fields were coloured purple by *Melampyrum arvense Riv* [crested cow-wheat] and *Rhananthus* [yellow rattle], growing more abundantly here than in any other place, made the ground look all yellow.

5 July

The farmers' botany is not to be despised, and the farmers, at least here, have their own names for almost all plants. I brought a good-natured farmer with me to the meadows, and he knew far more plants than I would ever have expected, and his names for them had often very nice origins.
Monorchis 'musk flower' [musk orchid] because of the form of the root and the smell of the flowers.
Anemone nemorosa 'Fagelblomma' [wood anemone], from the verb 'fuga', that is, to collect brushwood from the pastures, since it flowers when this is done.
Primula lutea 'cuckoo flower' [cowslip] flowers when the cuckoo calls.
Trifolium 'honey flower' [red clover].
Briza 'trembling-grass' [quaking grass].
Campanula 'thimble' [harebell].

1 Crested Cow-wheat
  Melampyrum cristatum
2 Yellow Rattle *Rhinanthus minor*
3 Harebell *Campanula rotundifolia*
4 Red Clover *Trifolium pratense*
5 Great Burnet *Sanguisorba officinalis*
6 Wild Carrot *Daucus carota*
7 Scarce Copper (male) *Heodes virgaureae*

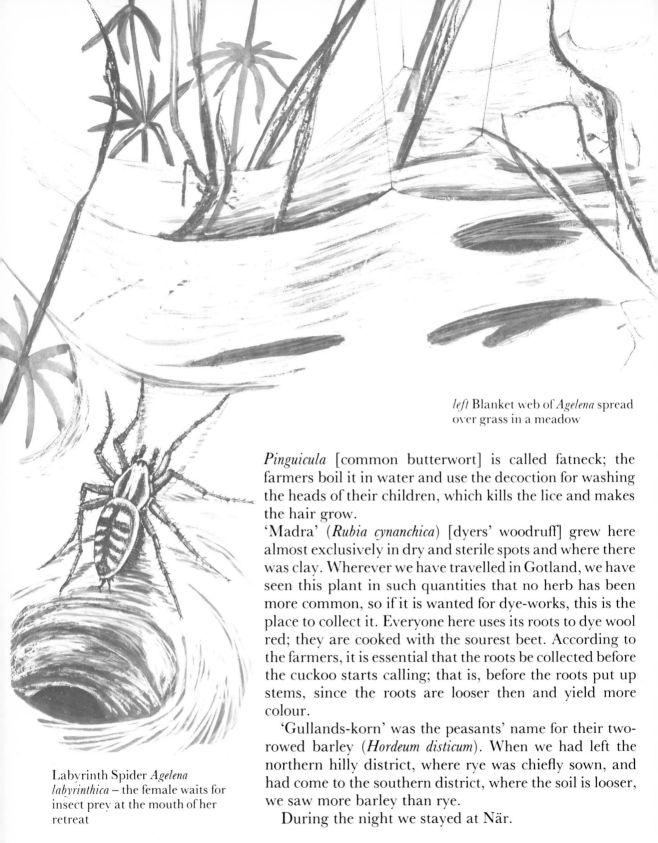

Pinguicula [common butterwort] is called fatneck; the farmers boil it in water and use the decoction for washing the heads of their children, which kills the lice and makes the hair grow.

'Madra' (*Rubia cynanchica*) [dyers' woodruff] grew here almost exclusively in dry and sterile spots and where there was clay. Wherever we have travelled in Gotland, we have seen this plant in such quantities that no herb has been more common, so if it is wanted for dye-works, this is the place to collect it. Everyone here uses its roots to dye wool red; they are cooked with the sourest beet. According to the farmers, it is essential that the roots be collected before the cuckoo starts calling; that is, before the roots put up stems, since the roots are looser then and yield more colour.

'Gullands-korn' was the peasants' name for their two-rowed barley (*Hordeum disticum*). When we had left the northern hilly district, where rye was chiefly sown, and had come to the southern district, where the soil is looser, we saw more barley than rye.

During the night we stayed at När.

Labyrinth Spider *Agelena labyrinthica* – the female waits for insect prey at the mouth of her retreat

86

Labyrinth spiders

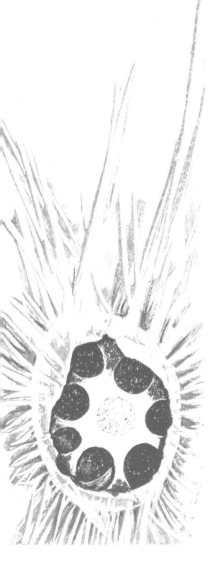

below Agelena's nest, cut away to expose the 'labyrinth' of cells inside. In the centre of this maze she lays her ball of eggs

Today our journey took us from Grottlingbo to Varmlingbo, through Fide, Öja and Hamra.

Large white spiders' webs covered the meadows. One side of the web was woven by the spider like a well or a cylindrical cavern on the ground, where he himself could reside and not be seen by birds or languish in the heat; as soon as the net was touched, he came up to look for his prey. The spider was an *Aranea abdomine fusco ovato* [*Agelena labyrinthica*]; the breast was of pale grey with three long pale stripes.

The flowers that now graced the meadows were above all: *Parnassia* [grass of Parnassus], *Filipendula* [dropwort], *Anthyllis* [kidney vetch], *Convolvulus* [field bindweed], *Agrimonia* [agrimony] and *Marrubium* [white horehound]. *Scabiosa: Morsus diaboli* [devilsbit scabious], the first autumn flower, raised its blue head, reminding the farmer that the time for mowing had come.

The grasshoppers were chirping in the meadows. We caught one of them, which is called 'wart-biter' (*Gryllus cauda ensifera recta* etc. [*Decticus verrucivorus*]; it is one of the biggest in Sweden; the female draws out her tail like a long sword. The male is entirely green and has four teeth in his tail and two pairs of short claws between the thighs. The wings, which rest on top of one another, are very remarkable in that towards the breast there are two membranes. When the grasshopper wants to make music for his beloved, he rubs his wings against each other, and the taut membrane makes the sound.

The mouths of both male and female consist of two pairs of jaws, of which the upper pair have many sharp teeth, but the lower pair are pointed and have no teeth. When the farmers have warts on their hands, they take such a grasshopper and put the wart to its mouth; the grasshopper bites the wart and spits a black corrosive liquid into it which makes the wart disappear.

The hedgehog's nest

Along the east coast towards Hoburgen, thrushes (*Turdi-pilulares*) [fieldfare] flew between the shrubs and chattered like jays; one of them was shot; it was as big as a blackbird; the head was iron-grey on the upper side and likewise on the rump above the tail; the feathers covering the back and wings were dark rust-coloured; the feathers in the tail and wings were blackish; the breast and the lower part of the throat were almost rust-coloured and besprinkled with black spots, of which those near the bill were small but more elongate.

Hoburgen, a mountain similar to Torsburgen, stands at the extreme south end of the land. Here we saw small moths *Phalaenaseticornis* etc. [*Eulamprotes wilkella*] in such great abundance that they threw themselves up like dust before our feet. They were among the smallest of moths, oblong and black, with four silvery transparent lines, of which the first was bent forwards, the second straight and the third and fourth bent towards the sides.

The crustacean *Cancer macrourus* etc. [*Gammarus locusta*] found in the water on the shore looked like a reddish minute shrimp. The snail *Cochlea testa pellucida* [*Helix balthica*] was also lying in the water by the shore; the animal was black and had two antennae looking like flat pointed ears.

Seaweed, *Ulva tubulosa ramosa compressa* [*Enteromorpha compressa*] lay abundantly on the shore where it had been thrown up; it was uneven, with many loops and cavities, and simple branches; it was pale, not green, and often no thicker than a thread.

In the afternoon we passed a little pine forest south of Varmlingbo, where we returned to spend the night.

There were hedgehogs here, and we caught a couple. The whole upper part of the body was thickly covered with spines; these were light grey or white, encircled with distinct small dark rings of which the outermost was the largest and darkest. The rest of the body and head, except

Common Hedgehog *Erinaceus europaeus* emerging from its daytime sleeping place. It uses its sense of smell to hunt mice, worms, insects and snails by night

the crown, was covered with light grey hair, as on a pig. The ears were rounded, the eyes small and black, the nose pointed. The fore-paws were like the claws of a bear with five clubbed toes. The female had eight teats and both male and female had a musk-like smell. The male and female hunted together at night and they were most often seen in the evenings. They build their nests in juniper bushes above the ground; these are of moss, rounded and hollow like a squirrel's nest; they are said to have usually four young. We had a remarkable proof of the fact that hedgehogs do eat meat; one of them devoured all the thrush described earlier, and left nothing but the thickest feathers. When we let it loose on the shore, it proved that it was not afraid of the water either; it went down to the sea at once and started to swim.

Runic tombstones

This day was used mainly for our mending, since our clothes were torn by bushes, rocks and much riding.

Anthyllis [kidney vetch] varied delightfully here in several colours – white, cream, yellow, red and pink. Together with this grew *Ononis* [rest harrow].

Wild carrots grew here as big and tall as dill. The root was white and smelled like ordinary carrot. The stalk was thinner and grooved.

Cerambyx cinereus etc. [*Leiopus nebulosus*] was a little irongrey beetle with black spots, denser at the wing base; it had a black band across the middle of the elytra.

The *Phalaena pectinicornis elinguis* [wood tiger; *Parasemia plantaginis*] is a beautiful but uncommon moth, with thin antennae and black wings with pale yellow veins, but the underwings are red with black spots.

Habbdum church is situated one and a half miles from Burgsvik. We arrived there at 9 pm. Although it was getting dark, we could read some runic stones in the churchyard, one of them with deeply cut letters. We had planned to stay here during the night, but a malignant fever had afflicted some people at the farm; thus we went on.

Darkness came upon us, so that we saw nothing except that the cats caught cockchafers and ate them. At midnight we arrived at Fardhem.

12 July

Hops are of two kinds, male and female. The female is the real hop, the buds of which are used for brewing. The male is called here 'Fuk-humble' (sterile hop), for it has no buds, only many small flowers. There was a hop yard of considerable size here, but there were only sterile hops in

Runic stone – many of these ancient inscribed stones are to be found in Gotland

opposite page
left to right Kidney Vetch *Anthyllis vulneraria*
Rest-harrow *Ononis repens*
Wild Carrot *Daucus carota*
Wood Tiger Moth *Parasemia plantaginis*

it. The owner had asked advice from old and wise farmers, who had told him that when the roots of the hops grow old and get thick bark, they only yield sterile hops, and that there was nothing to be done but to dig up the yard and replant it with the same roots, which would in turn give new fresh roots and good fruit. This was done, but the plants that grew up from the replanted roots still gave sterile hops, and the owner waited in vain for the real hops. The sterile hops come into the hop yard when the hops drop their seeds, which give rise to male and female plants in the same way as eggs from a hen give rise to cocks and hens; the sterile hops grow better and the female hops are easily suffocated, which can spoil the best hop yard.

Beehives were not seen here, although there were many on Öland. There was no heather here; the honey would be much whiter if bees were brought here. We were told of a bishop who had brought bees here formerly, but they had not survived, which should not be regarded as a precedent, since he lived in Visby, where the bees are exposed to a strong wind each day and the swarms have the opportunity to escape to the many old churches and towers.

We saw no flax on Gotland, and when we asked the people why they did not cultivate such an extremely useful plant, they answered that they had often sown a whole pailful of flax seeds in excellently prepared and manured soil, but got no more than a pound of flax, although it grew to more than 1 ell high; therefore they preferred to sow grain and sell it and buy their flax for the money thus received, which will give them three or four times as much of it. One could see from this that the farmers were very unaccustomed to this kind of cultivation.

Stora Karlsö Island

The silentness, the lack of news, here in the countryside is very great; newspapers do not come often, and except for two judges and one captain, there were no persons of standing on all Gotland, if those living in Visby were excluded.

The two Karlsö islands, the big one and the small one, are a quarter of a mile apart and less than half a mile from the mainland; both of them are very high and steep on all sides, resting on solid rock and surrounded by the sea.

Scolopendra teres pedibus utrinque CXX [*Julus sabulosus*] was 2 inches long, thick as the quill of a dove, smooth, grey, with two pale-yellow and even longitudinal stripes on the back; the body consisted of about sixty joints and every joint was grooved and paler at the margin. The feet were many, thin as hairs and light grey.

We found springs on Stora Karlsö with water which was much praised and tasted clean, but I did not dare drink it because of the worms on the bottom. These worms, *Gordius* or *Seta aquatica* [*Gordius aquaticus*], look like a horse-hair in shape and size and are pale with black head and tail. When they are cut in many pieces every piece moves, and the farmers in Småland told us that if these pieces are thrown into the water, every piece regenerates into a whole animal, which would seem incredible if it were not known that pieces of tapeworm can grow to full-sized animals after many fathoms of the worm have been torn off. If the eggs of *Gordius* enter into the stomach with the drinking water and are hatched there, they could easily bore into gut, liver, lungs and heart and cause strange and unknown diseases.

Plants left to right Fastigiate Gypsophila *Gypsophila fastigiata*; Artemisia *Artemisia rupestris*; Sheep's Fescue grass *Festuca ovina*

14 July

Stora Karlsö was very high, except for the south cape, with a horizontal infertile level on top. In this infertile field *Saponaria calcibus pentaphyllis* [fastigate gypsophila] grew everywhere and yet I have not seen it in Sweden or any botanical garden. This herb has been observed but never well described and hence it has been confused with other plants.

I will give its description here in order to make this clear to botanists. The root is perennial, as thick as a goose quill, and goes rather deep. The radical leaves form a tuft, as usual in pinks: they are linear, pressed down and somewhat thick. The stalk, ½ ell high, at first lies on the ground, but rises up when the flowers appear. The inflorescence terminates the stem and looks like a brush composed of flowers, of which the calyx is bell-shaped and divided to halfway down into five red lobes. The petals are five, broad, oblong, blunt, outspread. The filaments are 10, white, as long as the petals; after one day five bend back and next day the other five also bend back. The anthers are also white. The ovary is globular. Styles two, thread-like, as long as the stamens.

Artemisia foliis pinnatis etc. [wormwood: *Artemisia rupestris*] was found on the northern part of Stora Karlsö, directly below the place where an ash tree stood. The plant was withered and similar to *Abrotanum campestre* [breckland mugwort] which grew here too; but when one examined it more closely, this was found to be the rarest of all plants we saw on the journey, or maybe a completely new plant. A special distinguishing feature of this plant is that the flowers are big and globose, looking like round pills, which makes it easy to differentiate from others. I brought it with me to the university garden in Uppsala, where it has survived the winters and spreads by its roots, but because it flowers late it has ripened no seeds for several years.

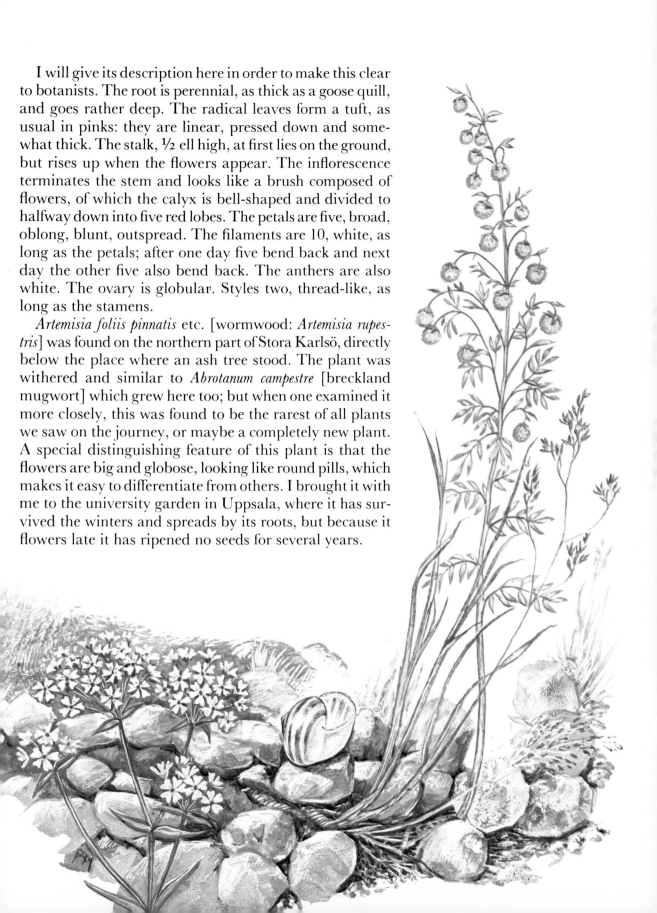

Lilla Karlsö Island

From Stora Karlsö we went to Lilla Karlsö by boat. As soon as we came out on the water, gulls and sea birds started to fly about us with much screeching and screaming. *Alca, rostri sulcis quatuor* [razorbills] flew rapidly around the boat several times without fear, and although we shot at the birds, they did not go away but became ever more eager to fly above our heads. This bird is very rare in Sweden; it is as big as a raven, heavy and fleshy. It builds its nest in the highest and steepest rock crevices, where it lays only one egg and if this one is removed, it immediately lays another one. Razorbills are away in winter, but return on the first day of May, and leave their summer quarters at the time of the St Laurence's festival (10 August).

The black guillemot was a bird that we only saw flying; and it was similar to the razorbill but smaller. The farmers told us that it also walks upright, has red feet and is red under the tail. The breast is black, not white as on the razorbill. It was said to have two eggs and build its nest in the crevices, but never more than 2 fathoms above the water.

A sparrow that was almost black was seen on the north side of the island, but it was impossible to shoot it; perhaps it was a shearwater (*Procellaria*).

22 July

We tried every day to leave Gotland, but had to stay here like prisoners because no ship was ready to leave – and to trust one's life to the mail boat, which was small, frail, old and unsound, and, still worse, to its captain, would have been very adventurous. When we nevertheless had to make a deal with him, I do not know what confused him, since he failed us and left without our knowing. If those who are responsible for this mail transport would arrange matters in another way, they would do the inhabitants a great service.

24 July

At last we found a ship; thus we said goodbye to the gentlemen of Visby who had almost competed with each other in their cordiality towards us. Night fell, but as the sailors were not ready, we could do nothing but wait.

25 July

At half past five in the morning we went on board. At the risk of our lives we left the harbour in a furious sea, our friends and Visby disappeared, the Karlsö islands appeared, a northern wind started to whistle, the waves raged, the ship was thrown between the roaring billows, Gotland disappeared, my companions became sea-sick, the rigging burst, our hearts filled with despair and we committed our fate to God's hands . . .

Black Guillemots *Cepphus grylle*
breed in scattered colonies in rock crevices sometimes quite far up inlets. Their eggs are white, blotched with brown or grey spots

Linnaean Classification
by William T. Stearn

Although Linnaeus has been declared a pioneer ecologist, a pioneer plant-geographer, a pioneer dendrochronologist, a pioneer evolutionist, a botanical pornographer and sexualist, and much else, the most influential and useful of his contributions to biology undoubtedly is his successful introduction of consistent binomial specific nomenclature for plants and animals, even though this achievement was but an incidental by-product of his vast encyclopaedic task of providing in a concise convenient form the means of recognizing and recording their genera and species. Use of two-word names (binomials) for individual kinds, with one word applicable to a whole group of objects but the other word limiting the name to a single member of the group, is a very old and almost universal manner of naming, rooted in the need to distinguish the general and the particular, but Linnaeus was the first deliberately to apply binomials to plants and animals uniformly. In all he coined Latin or Latin-form internationally usable names for roughly 4,400 species of animals and 7,700 species of plants, linking these names with descriptions, diagnoses, or illustrations which made evident and stabilized their application. His *Species Plantarum* (1753), together with his *Genera Plantarum* (5th ed., 1754), has consequently been accepted by international agreement among botanists as the starting-point for botanical nomenclature in general. Hence botanical names published before 1753 have no standing in modern nomenclature unless they were adopted by Linnaeus in 1753 or later or by subsequent authors and such names are designated as 'pre-Linnaean', including those published by Linnaeus himself before 1753! His *Systema Naturae*, vol. 1 (10th ed., 1758) has similarly been internationally accepted by zoologists as the starting-point for the modern scientific naming of animals. But for these works and their lasting nomenclatural status Linnaeus would not now be remembered and receive so much biographical attention when his contemporaries of equal if not higher intellectual powers, though of less self-sacrificing industry, are mostly forgotten. Taxonomic botanists and zoologists, especially those concerned with European, North American, and Indian plants and animals, have continually to refer back to the works of Linnaeus when checking names. Unless, however, Linnaean methods and the aims and history, the procedures and terminology of these Linnaean works are understood, they are likely to be misinterpreted and Linnaeus's scientific names may be misapplied through erroneous typification, as indeed some have been. The following notes, mostly brought together from more detailed publications of mine, are intended as an introduction to these technical Linnaean matters.

The basis of Linnaeus's achievement was his strong sense of order. It is evident in all his publications and it much impressed his students. Thus the entomologist J. C. Fabricius, who attended Linnaeus's lectures on natural classification in 1764, wrote in 1780 that 'his greatest asset was the co-ordinated arrangement which his thoughts took. Everything which he said and did was orderly, was systematic, and I can hardly believe that Europe will produce a more systematical genius.' In the creation of the methods he used, his ill-fated friend Peter Artedi seemingly contributed as much as Linnaeus himself, but after Artedi's death in 1735 their application to the three kingdoms of Nature fell upon Linnaeus alone. Reared in a pious atmosphere, spared from death on his travels, always strongly egoistic, Linnaeus could excusably believe himself God's chosen instrument for revealing in an orderly way the divinely ordered works of Creation, and he did not spare himself in that task. The first part of it was the classification of organisms into major groups.

Clariſ: LINNÆI.M.D.
METHODUS plantarum SEXUALIS
in SISTEMATE NATURÆ
deſcripta

Lugd. bat: 1736

G.D.EHRET. Palat-heidelb:
fecit & edidit

above A page from the original 'Sexual System of Nature' illustrated by Ehret (see pages 100-101)

Linnaeus's Sexual System of Classification

In the arrangement of genera Linnaeus's *Species Plantarum* (1753) and *Genera Plantarum* (1754) follow the 'Sexual System' of classification which he introduced to the learned world in the first edition of his *Systema Naturae* (1735), by setting it forth as a key, *Clavis systematis sexualis* (see pp 100-101). It is a basically simple but ingenious arithmetical system, whereby the genera are grouped into twenty-four classes according to the number of the stamens (together with their relative lengths, their distinctness or fusion, their occurrence in the same flower as the pistil or their separation in unisexual flowers, or their apparent absence), the Monandria having one stamen, the Diandria two stamens, the Triandria three stamens and so on; it ends with the Cryptogamia whose reproductive habits were not then understood. Within each class the genera are arranged into smaller groups or *orders* acccording to the numbers of pistils, the Monogynia having one pistil, the Digynia two pistils, the Trigynia three pistils, and so on. Thus, despite its alluring name, this system is based, as Sachs emphasized, on exactly those characters of the androecium and gynoecium which are least important as regards their sexual function.

97

Linnaeus learned from Johan S. Rothman when at school at Växjö the importance attributed by Tournefort to flower-form as a basis of classification. He also became acquainted with Vaillant's views on the sexual functions of the flower-parts, although he never saw Vaillant's memoir *Sermo de Structura Florum* (1718, reissued 1727 and 1728) until years later, and soon he was able to place every plant growing around Stenbrohult in its class according to the Tourneftortian system. His own system thus rested in the first place upon an intimate acquaintance with the comparatively limited flora of a Swedish parish. The University Botanic Garden brought other plants of the temperate flora to his attention at Uppsala. Here in 1729 the attempt of a fellow-student, the brilliant ill-fated Petrus Artedi, to work out a new classification of the *Umbelliferae* aroused in Linnaeus a desire to do the same for all plants. Although he may have deduced his system from observations on the number of parts in many flowers examined, it seems more likely he was led to it by an *a priori* belief that parts so fundamental for the reproduction of plants would be equally so for their classification. His Lapland journey gave him the opportunity for classifying with its aid an arctic flora. In Holland he was able to test it on plants from the tropics and to modify it into a convenient working tool for the world's flora as a whole. Thus, as happened several times in the career of Linnaeus, what might have been a handicap turned ultimately to his advantage. Confronted at the beginning with a tropical flora full of 'legions of monstrous Plants, enough to confound all the methods of Botany ever hitherto thought upon' (as a Scottish botanist, James Wallace, in 1700 described Darien as possessing), their leaves, flowers and fruits bewilderingly diverse, the number of species incalculable, Linnaeus would probably have never hit upon so simple a key to their grouping as his 'Sexual System'.

The dramatic metaphorical form in which Linnaeus published his system based on the 'loves of the plants' was better suited to the temper and manners of the 18th and 19th century, though even in that robust period it did not escape criticism. Thus Johann Amman wrote to Sloane on 6 September 1736 about 'some systematical tables concerning Natural History, composed by Dr Linnaeus' and doubted 'very much if any Botanist will follow his lewd method.' In 1737 the St Petersburg academician Johann G. Siegesbeck attacked it harshly on the ground that 'such loathsome harlotry' ('scortationes quasi detestabiles') as several males to one female would never have been permitted in the vegetable kingdom by the Creator and asked how anyone could teach without offence 'so licentious a method' ('methodum talem lascivam') to studious youth. He is remembered today only through the unpleasant small-flowered weed which Lin-

Round-leaved Wintergreen *Pyrola rotundifolia*, which has one pistil and 10 stamens – one wife and 10 husbands

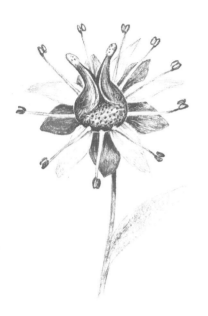

Yellow Mountain Saxifrage
Saxifraga aizoides, which has two
pistils and 10 stamens – two wives
and 10 husbands

naeus named *Sigesbeckia*. The subjects of King George II were amused rather than shocked by these revelations. Botany as simplified by Linnaeus passed easily enough into drawing rooms where Hogarth's prints were admired and the novels of Fielding and Smollet read. As Croizat (1945) has remarked, 'by a bold stroke of the pen the nebulous world of plants was made to act like husbands and wives in unconcerned freedom and everybody prepared to grasp the meaning of Monoecia and Dioecia, Syngenesia and Polygamia without effort'. It was an early 19th-century reviewer, not an 18th-century one, who stated that no botanical text-book should bring 'the blush of injured modesty to the cheeks of the innocent fair; this we consider most important'. By then, however, the Linnaean system was rapidly losing popularity and being superseded by more natural systems.

Linnaeus knew very well that the system outlined above was an artificial one. Its purpose being to enable botanists to determine plants without having a teacher at hand, it brought together plants which, though agreeing in the number of their stamens and pistils, were very different in many other particulars. As Amman asked Linnaeus, 'What affinity is there, except in the number of their stamens, between *Valeriana* and *Cyperus*, *Persicaria* and *Campanula*, *Gentiana*, *Ribes*, and *Angelica* etc?' Linnaeus, like Ray before him, sought for a natural system more expressive of their true affinities, a system based on the relationship between all parts. He even outlined what he thought might be such a system, publishing a first draft, 'fragmenta methodi naturalis', in his *Classes Plantarum* (1738). He stated his more mature views in two series of lectures, the first in 1764 to his students Ferber, Fabricius, Zoega, Meyer and Kuhn who had come from Philadelphia, the second in 1771 to Giseke, Vahl, Edinger and Tislef. From his own notes and those of Fabricius, Giseke published in 1792 Linnaeus's *Praelectiones in Ordines naturales Plantarum*. Many of the groups there defined have passed into modern classifications almost unchanged, some retaining their Linnaean names as *Cucurbitaceae*, *Papilionaceae*, *Palmae* and *Compositae*, although nomenclatural changes have disguised others. Thus Linnaeus's order Calamariae corresponds to the family *Cyperaceae*, his Gramina to the *Gramineae*, his Ensatae largely to the *Iridaceae*, his Scitamineae largely to the *Zingiberaceae*, his Spathaceae largely to the *Amaryllidaceae*, his Coronariae largely to the *Liliaceae*, his Bicornes largely to the *Ericaceae*, his Caryophyllei to the *Caryophyllaceae*, his Multisiliquae largely to the *Ranunculaceae*, his Luridae largely to the *Solanaceae*, his Contortae largely to the *Asclepiadaceae* and *Apocynaceae*, his Senticosae and Pomaceae to the *Rosaceae*, his Columniferae largely to the *Malvaceae*, his Sepiariae to the *Oleaceae*, his Umbellatae largely to the *Umbelliferae*, his Stellatae largely to the *Rubiaceae*. Linnaeus expressed the relation of the two types of classification in an aphorism at the end of the sixth edition (1764) of the *Genera Plantarum*:

> Ordines naturales valent de natura plantarum.
> Artificiales in diagnosi plantarum.

VEGETABLE KINGDOM
KEY OF THE SEXUAL SYSTEM

MARRIAGES of PLANTS.
Florescence.

PUBLIC MARRIAGES.
Flowers visible to every one.

IN ONE BED.
Husband and wife have the same bed.
All the flowers hermaphrodite: stamens and pistils in the same flower.

WITHOUT AFFINITY.
Husbands not related to each other.
Stamens not joined together in any part.

WITH EQUALITY.
All the males of equal rank.
Stamens have no determinate proportion of length.

1. ONE MALE.	7. SEVEN MALES.
2. TWO MALES.	8. EIGHT MALES.
3. THREE MALES.	9. NINE MALES.
4. FOUR MALES.	10. TEN MALES.
5. FIVE MALES.	11. TWELVE MALES.
6. SIX MALES.	12. TWENTY MALES.
	13. MANY MALES.

WITH SUBORDINATION
Some males above others.
Two stamens are always lower than the others.

14. TWO POWERS.	15. FOUR POWERS.

WITH AFFINITY
Husbands related to each other.
Stamens cohere with each other, or with the pistil.

16. ONE BROTHERHOOD.	19. CONFEDERATE
17. TWO BROTHERHOODS.	MALES
18. MANY BROTHERHOODS.	20. FEMININE MALES.

IN TWO BEDS.
Husband and wife have separate beds.
Male flowers and female flowers in the same species.

21. ONE HOUSE.	23. POLYGAMIES.
22. TWO HOUSES.	

CLANDESTINE MARRIAGES.
Flowers scarce visible to the naked eye.

24. CLANDESTINE MARRIAGES.

The classes of Linnaeus's se[x]
system of classification, as
illustrated in Ehret's origina[l]
plate, 1736

A, 1. *Monandria*; B, 2. *Diandr[ia]*
C, 3. *Triandria*; D, 4. *Tetrandr[ia]*
E, 5. *Pentandria*; F, 6. *Hexandr[ia]*
G, 7. *Heptandria*; H, 8. *Octan[dria]*
I, 9. *Enneandria*; K, 10. *Deca[ndria]*

100

It fell to others, having first identified their material by Linnaean methods, to elaborate more natural systems practical enough for purposes of identification to supersede his admittedly artificial one.

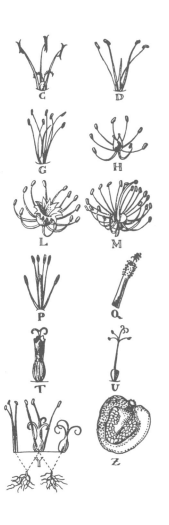

L, 11. *Dodecandria*;
M, 12. *Icosandria*; N, 13. *Polyandria*;
O, 14. *Didynamia*;
P, 15. *Tetradynamia*;
Q, 16. *Monadelphia*;
R, 17. *Diadelphia*;
S, 18. *Polyadelphia*; T, 19. *Syngenesia*;
U, 20. *Gynandria*; V, 21. *Monoecia*;
X, 22. *Dioecia*; Y, 23. *Polygamia*;
Z, 24. *Cryptogamia*.

REGNUM VEGETABILE
CLAVIS SYSTEMATIS SEXUALIS
NUPTIAE PLANTARUM.
Actus generationis incolarum Regni vegetabilis.
Florescentia.
PUBLICAE.
Nuptiae, omnibus manifestae, aperte celebrantur.
Flores unicuique visibiles.
MONOCLINIA.
Mariti & uxores uno eodemque thalamo gaudent.
Flores omnes hermaphroditi: stamina cum pistillis in eodem flore.
DIFFINITAS.
Mariti inter se non cognati.
Stamina nulla sua parte connata inter se sunt.
INDIFFERENTISMUS.
Mariti absque subordinatione.
Stamina longitudine indeterminata.

1. MONANDRIA.	7. HEPTANDRIA.
2. DIANDRIA.	8. OCTANDRIA.
3. TRIANDRIA.	9. ENNEANDRIA.
4. TETRANDRIA.	10. DECANDRIA.
5. PENTANDRIA.	11. DODECANDRIA.
6. HEXANDRIA.	12. ICOSANDRIA.
	13. POLYANDRIA.

SUBORDINATIO.
Mariti certi reliquis praeferuntur.
Stamina duo semper reliquis breviora sunt.
14. DIDYNAMIA.   15. TETRADYNAMIA.
AFFINITAS.
Mariti propinqui & cognati sunt.
Stamina coherent vel inter se, vel cum pistillo.

16. MONADELPHIA.	19. SYNGENESIA.
17. DIADELPHIA.	20. GYNANDRIA.
18. POLYADELPHIA.	

DICLINIA duplex thalamus.
Mariti & Feminae distinctis thalamis gaudent.

21. MONOECIA.	23. POLYGAMIA.
22. DIOECIA.	

CLANDESTINAE.
Nuptiae clam instituuntur.
Flores oculis nostris nudis vix conspiciuntur.
24. CRYPTOGAMIA.

101

Glossary

Alternate (of leaves) arranged alternately on opposite sides of the stem

Anther the organ at the top of the stamen which contains the pollen grains

Arborescent growing like a tree

Bifurcated (of stems) branching equally into two parts

Calyx the outermost part of flowers, the sepals, often united at the base to form a tube

Capsule (in mosses) the 'fruit', the organ which contains the spores

Corolla the part of flowers formed by the petals, often joined at the base or through their length to form a tube

Deciduous (of trees) having leaves which fall each year in autumn; not evergreen

Diadelphous with stamens joined by the filaments (the lower parts of the stamens) into two bundles

Dilated widened

Entire (of leaves) with edges not serrated, undulating or otherwise divided

Filament the stalk-like process which supports the anthers

Flexuose (of stems) wavy, zig-zag

Glabrous (of leaves and stems) smooth, without hairs

Globose spherical

Imbricate(d) with petals, leaves or scales overlapping

Inflorescence the complete flower head

Lanceolate (of leaves) lance-shaped, tapering towards the tip and broadest two-thirds along the length

Obtuse (of leaves) blunt ended

Ovary part of the flower below the style in which the ovules (egg cells) become fertilized by pollen and develop into seeds

Ovate (of leaves) egg-shaped

Pendulous hanging from a stalk as, e.g., male hazel catkins

Perennial living for a period exceeding two years

Petal the (usually) brightly coloured elements in the flower, situated within the calyx. Petals form the corolla

Pinnate (of leaves) divided into leaflets on opposite sides of a stalk

Pistil the female organ of a flower, comprising ovary, style and stigma

Quadrangular (of stems) having four corners, square in cross-section

Reflexed (of petals or leaves) bent as, e.g., cyclamen

Sepals the outermost parts of a flower, often green, though sometimes brightly coloured. They are divided more or less to the base into two or more segments

Septum membranous division often found in ovaries

Serrature tooth-like notch on a leaf margin

Spawn (of fish and amphibians) the eggs laid by the female and fertilized by the male

Specific characteristic of a species and only of that species

Spore (of ferns, mosses, fungi, etc.) the microscopic, asexual fruiting body, usually produced in huge numbers, and dispersed by wind or water

Stamen the male organ of a flower, comprising the filament and anther

Stigma sticky top of the style, the female organ of the flower, which receives the pollen

Stipule a small, leaf-like organ found at the base of the leaf-stalk

Style tube connecting the stigma and the ovary, down which pollen passes from the stigma to the ovary

Tripartite divided into three parts

Index

Conversion of old measurements from the original text

Old measure	metric	imperial
1 mile (Swedish)	10.7 km	6⅔ miles
1 fathom	1.8 metres	72 inches
1 ell	0.60 metres	24 inches
1 spann	0.20 metres	8 inches

Further reading and sources

Unfortunately most of Linnaeus's works are not obtainable in English translation. For those wishing to go deeply into the subject, the Transactions *and* Proceedings *of the Linnaean Society in London are invaluable. The publications listed below are some of the more accessible in the English language.*

Blunt, W. (with the assistance of W.T. Stearn), The Compleat Naturalist: A Life of Linnaeus, *London, 1971*

Blunt, W., 'Linnaeus and Botany' (Linnaeus's systems of botanical classification and nomenclature, for the layman), History Today, *London, Feb. 1971*

Gourlie, Norah, The Prince of Botanists, *London, 1953*

Hagberg, Knut, Carl Linnaeus *(tr. Alan Blair), London, 1952*

Jackson, B.D., Linnaeus *(condensed version of standard biography by T.M. Fries), London, 1923*

Linnaeus, Carl, Lachesis Lapponica *(tr. Carl Troilus, ed. J.E. Smith), London, 1792*

Linnaeus's Öland and Gotland Journey 1741, *translated by Marie Åsberg and William T. Stearn, with an Introduction by William T. Stearn, London, 1973*

Stearn, W.T., 'An Introduction to the Species Plantarum *', prefixed to the Ray society's edition of Linnaeus's* Species Plantarum, *London, 1957*

Original Linnaean material is mainly housed in the following institutions: The British Museum (Natural History); the Linnaean Society of London; the Botanical and Zoological Museums, Uppsala; the Natural History Museum, Stockholm; the Institut de France, Paris.

Wij sego gienom stranden åtskillige kallågure, som bliga
5. alnar höga at de bredh at at bygga sine ugnarne,
inåt lutade alt mere at manskaden i jorden dragare,
på det draden at aldrin mattta lättare koma in: Wij
sego de öfverste stenarne i ugnars halt hiete sisune
med Mogal öfverdragen: follas hade af det
wart sallasste, men då wit togo hate stenarne
war det at hiett sal aldrali calcareum som sitt
sisom flores sulphuris öfver stenarne at sorelshen
på ingare. Stneidnotten til kallar wore ytterste
horaten af strenden, hirerofs kallan wordt med
ringa moda, andefs med kofot, harundre; de fle
forna skildes frå hirarandra, langs Orthocerothes
så tätt som agnar i groft bröd, at Gud wet
hurer så manger dius solad bagitt. Huridenad
egar at annat petrificat silsgatarn, som sig ut til
en valvula af Echinno, ofter stor som farta harudem, sig
at som half-månad med 2. sulcis parallelis at åtskilli
ge strig transverst.
Uti faretekerne af Orthocerothes sig man sat-
ekrystaller, med figuren sictri, del irllanoss til sin
apex som wart mer utsporedt dru ordinairt, colu-
mnam sago man intet til.

Staunsollan som het thiört med egar sten. under sit
lieofunde siedach stadigt på strumgen fast sielsern orlande
halle sommarne.

Härt fanst en coccionella bland de stors ene öfgena sig
på klarod med langa pandter at gnäkes hiete, sioilte
hiete slacter i figaren med hersteppermenes: imunder
war son at klarod
Et syste härifran sego wij wid Lenstbergen en Rhamay
Catarticus den storste wij nagonsin wart. husarer om
Ri